Building Strategy and Performance Through Time

Building Strategy and Performance Through Time

The Critical Path

Kim Warren

Building Strategy and Performance Through Time

First published by Vola Press Ltd., London 2005

Published in 2009 by
Business Expert Press, LLC
222 East 46th Street, New York, NY 10017
www.businessexpertpress.com

ISBN-13: 978-1-60649-037-2 (paperback)
ISBN-10: 1-60649-037-0 (paperback)

ISBN-13: 978-1-60649-038-9 (e-book)
ISBN-10: 1-60649-038-9 (e-book)

DOI 10.4128/9781606490389

A publication in the Business Expert Press Strategic Management collection

Collection ISSN (print) forthcoming
Collection ISSN (electronic) forthcoming

Cover design by Artistic Group—Monroe, NY
Interior design by Scribe, Inc.

First edition: April 2009

10 9 8 7 6 5 4 3 2 1

Printed in the United States of America.

Abstract

The fundamental challenge facing business leaders is to drive performance into the future—the *dynamics* of strategy. To tackle this effectively, they need a clear understanding of what *causes* performance to improve or deteriorate and what power they have to change this trajectory for the better. Without this understanding, they risk making poor choices about their future—failing to exploit promising opportunities, pursuing unachievable aims, or falling victim to competitive and other threats.

Building Strategy and Performance Through Time sets the agenda for building business strategy in powerful, actionable, and accessible terms. It gives executives clear frameworks for answering three fundamental questions:

- *Why* is our business performance following its current path?
- *Where* is it going if we carry on as we are?
- *How* can we design a robust strategy to transform this future?

The existing strategy tools most widely used help guide management's choices about *where* to compete—which customers to serve, with what products and services, and how to deliver those products and services to those customers effectively and profitably. While this choice is important, it is not often changed in any fundamental way; having found a reasonably strong and profitable position on these issues, few firms will, or should, set off in a new direction. But there is still much to be done to *deliver* that strategy, powerfully and sustainably over time. Many decisions need to be made, continually and holistically, across all functions of the business and adapted as conditions change from month to month and year to year. Pricing, product development, marketing, hiring, service levels, and other decisions cannot be made in isolation but must take into account other choices being made, elsewhere and at different times.

Building Strategy and Performance Through Time explains a reliable, practical method, known as *strategy dynamics*, that creates a living picture of how an enterprise actually works and delivers performance. This picture shows exactly where the levers are that management controls and how to choose what to do, when, and how much, to accomplish your specific goals. It shows, too, how the same approach can be used to defeat competitors, cope with other outside forces, and keep delivering performance.

Keywords

Strategic management, business strategy, strategy implementation, competitive strategy, strategy dynamics, business model

Contents

Introduction. 1

Chapter 1: Performance Through Time .3

Chapter 2: Resources: Vital Drivers of Performance 19

Chapter 3: Resources and Bathtub Behavior. 31

Chapter 4: Driving the Machine: Handling
          Interdependence Between Resources. 45

Chapter 5: Building and Managing the Strategic Architecture 65

Chapter 6: You Need Quality Resources as Well as Quantity 83

Chapter 7: Managing Rivalry for Customers
          and Other Resources 97

Chapter 8: Intangible Resources and Capabilities. 111

Going Forward. 133

References 135

Index 137

Introduction

The defining challenge facing business leaders is to develop and drive performance into the future. For commercial firms, this generally means building profits and growing the value of the business. Although their focus may be on nonfinancial outcomes, public services, voluntary groups, and other not-for-profit organizations share the same central challenge—continually improving their performance. When the causes of performance through time are not understood, management has difficulty making the right decisions about important issues. Worse, entire organizations are led into ill-chosen strategies for their future.

To overcome these problems, leaders need the means to answer three basic questions:

1. Why is business performance following its current path?
2. Where are current policies, decisions, and strategy leading us?
3. How can future prospects be improved?

These questions are the starting point for this book.

The key to achieving business success is the ability to develop and sustain critical resources and capabilities, leveraging what we have today to grow more of what we will need tomorrow. This book explains the journey your organization takes through time as it builds this portfolio of vital resources. It provides innovative ideas that enable readers to answer the three questions and develop a sustainable winning strategy.

The approach described here is based on strategy dynamics (Warren, 2008), a rigorous, fact-based method for developing and managing strategy. The underlying science is known as system dynamics, which originated at the Massachusetts Institute of Technology in the 1960s (Forrester, 1961; Sterman, 2000). Strategy dynamics explain why the performance of an organization has changed through time in the way that it has, provide estimates of where it is likely to go in the future, and allow management to design strategies and policies to improve that future path. Strategy dynamics achieve this by building an integrated, fact-based picture of how the resources of your business are developing through time, driven by mutual interdependence, management policies, external opportunities, and constraints.

This book has been written in a compact and easy-to-read style to help managers quickly understand the underlying causes of strategic challenges so that they can take action to improve performance. It uses clear examples to show how things can go well if managers have a firm grasp of the changing resources in their business, or badly if this perspective is missing. It describes practical techniques for developing a dynamic, time-based picture of a range of challenges. It includes

- **a clear overview at the start of each chapter** setting out the issues and techniques to be explained;
- **action checklists** highlighting practical considerations to help ensure that the approach is applied successfully;
- **worked examples, diagrams, and tips on doing it right**, showing how the techniques and ideas can be implemented to uncover new insights and benefit your entire organization.

Traveling the critical path to organizational success is a challenging and fascinating journey. This book provides a practical, in-depth guide to help you along the way. If you would like to understand and discuss these techniques in more detail, I would be delighted to hear from you at http://www.strategydynamics.com/forum or visit to my blog at http://www.kimwarren.com.

CHAPTER 1

Performance Through Time

Overview

The biggest challenge facing business leaders is to understand and drive performance into the future while improving long-term profits. Executives in nonprofit organizations have performance aims too, though they may not be financial. To tackle this challenge, leaders need good answers to three basic questions: why the business's performance is following its current path, where current policies and strategy will lead, and how the future can be altered for the better.

This chapter will do the following:

- **clarify these questions** and explain the contribution that a sound approach to strategy can make
- **explain why performance through time is so critical**
- **outline some limitations of existing strategy tools** that explain why few senior managers use them
- **give you practical techniques** for developing a time-based picture of the challenges you face

The Challenge for Business Leaders

Your organization's history is fundamental to its future. What you can achieve tomorrow depends on what you have today, and what you have today is the total of everything you have built up, and held on to, in the past. This is true even for new ventures when the entrepreneur brings experience, credibility, and contacts to bear on creating the new business.

It also holds true for nonprofit activities: voluntary groups, government services, and nongovernmental organizations (NGOs). They too can only achieve what is possible with their current resources, and if more resources are needed then existing ones must be used to get them. A charity will not appeal to many new donors, for example, unless it has built a reputation.

When the causes of performance through time are not understood, organizations make poor choices about their future. They embark on plans they cannot achieve and fail to assemble what they need in order to achieve even those plans that *might* be feasible. The catalog of failed initiatives, in every sector and through all time, would make a thick book indeed. These failures are costly not only in money but also in terms of wasted and damaged human potential. The better news is that organizations are often capable of far *more* than they imagine, if only they choose objectives well and piece together the necessary elements.

Improving an organization's performance is not just a matter for top management. Given the right tools, everyone with influence over the way in which any part of their enterprise functions can make a difference. Challenges may be focused on an individual department or span the whole organization; they may range from very small to truly huge; and they may call for urgent measures or a long-term approach. This book focuses on the *content* of strategy—what the strategy actually is—in contrast to the equally important issues of the *process* by which strategy happens in organizations (Mintzberg, Lampel, Quinn, & Ghoshal, 1997).

The Importance of Time

The following cases illustrate organization-wide challenges with long-term implications but short-term imperatives for action. The scale of each issue is important, and the cases highlight the time path over which strategic challenges evolve and resources develop or decline. Ensuring that these changes play out at the right speed is vital.

The starting point for the approach that we will develop in later chapters is shown in Exhibit 1.1.

These time charts display three important characteristics:

1. A numerical scale (registered users, revenues)
2. A time scale (7 years of history to 2007)
3. The time path (how the situation changes over that time scale)

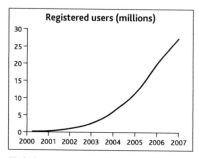
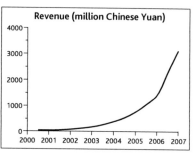

Exhibit 1.1. Alibaba.com Growth and Alternative Futures

Case Example: Alibaba.com

We are used to thinking of the goliaths of the Internet age, such as Google, Amazon, and eBay, as unassailable leaders in their fields, but Chinese upstart Alibaba.com showed that eBay, for one, could be beaten to a massive opportunity, given a careful focus.

From the most humble resources—just $60,000 in capital and 18 poorly paid colleagues—the founder, Jack Ma, laid out a vision for what Alibaba could become. Although highly speculative, the vision was sufficiently promising to attract venture funding and some big-name advisers to his board.

The business focused on helping smaller Chinese firms that wanted to grow business globally but found existing options to be too expensive. The key proposition was to connect such companies to similarly small and midsized buyers around the world. In spite of the apparent potential and easier access to larger firms, Alibaba maintained this focus on small and medium-size enterprises (SMEs). It also stuck to offering the simple service of connecting buyers and sellers rather than getting involved in other complementary activities.

A critical issue right at the start was to get sellers and buyers to sign up. Not only did this mean offering the core service at no charge but also dealing with the fear of technology among this segment of target users by making the Web site ultrasimple to use. In 2000, the company started selling advertising space and research reports on its sellers, but revenues were still tiny, at just $1 million, and no profits were being made.

In 2001, Alibaba started charging for its services, though still at a low rate of $3,000 per year. However, by this time the service's visibility and reputation were so strong that membership kept on climbing, passing the 1 million mark in 2002.

From this focused start, the company was able to extend its activities in several directions, first establishing a within-China service in the local language and then making a major thrust to develop business-to-consumer (B2C) and consumer-to-consumer (C2C) services. By 2007 the group was serving 24 million users and had effectively sealed victory over eBay, which exited the market.

These three features ensure that the charts provide a clear view of the challenge, and allow further details to be added later. This particular example happens to focus directly on a critical resource—registered users—and clarifies the absolute numbers: much more useful than derived ratios such as market share or abstract notions such as competitive advantage. Often, management's concern will be directed at the financial *consequences*—in other words, revenues and profits.

Understanding the history of decisions that have already been made is essential, as they are driving the business's trajectory into the future. Past additions to the services offered and to the customer groups targeted brought the business to its state in 2007. Success or failure in the company's future choices on these and other issues will determine its trajectory forward from that point in time.

Exhibit 1.2 shows preferred and feared futures for Blockbuster. Even with the best fortune and skilled management, the company will do well to sustain revenues and remain profitable, and it is hard to see how it might avoid closing more stores. Services such as Netflix are not the only threat—by 2008, increases in communications speed and data processing power were finally making the fully online delivery of movies and other content a practical reality. This threatened a still faster decline in store-based rental income. Note, by the way, that for Blockbuster to engage in online delivery of movies does *not* remove the challenge that this innovation creates for its stores and postal business. Even if it were successful in that initiative, someone would still have the challenge of managing the

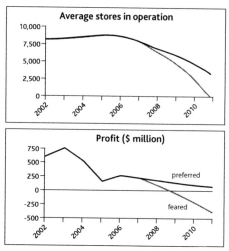

Exhibit 1.2. Alternative Futures for Blockbuster Inc.

Case Example: Blockbuster Inc.

Not all strategic challenges are so happily able to focus on sustaining spectacular growth in business activity and financial rewards. Other cases pose substantial threats, where the best that strategic management may be able to achieve is to resist decline or even closure.

Blockbuster Inc., from its startup and early growth in the late 1980s, effectively defined and dominated the market for renting movies to watch at home. Up to 1995, sales and profits climbed ever upward, driven by aggressive expansion of the company's store network, both owned and franchised, voracious acquisition of smaller chains, and entry into many new country markets. From 1995, it proved hard to sustain profitability, and by 2000 pressures on revenues and profits escalated sharply with the launch of Netflix.com, a service that allowed consumers to order movies on the Internet for postal delivery and return. With the new convenience this offered consumers, and without the costly burden of store real estate and staff, Netflix was able to offer very attractive prices and soon started to steal consumers from Blockbuster.

Soon other providers such as Amazon offered a similar service, and Blockbuster found itself fighting for its life. It had no choice but to offer a comparable postal service, adding to the erosion of store revenues in spite of the company's best efforts to make a positive advantage of the combined channels. As revenues suffered, marginal stores began to lose money, and closures became inevitable.

declining revenue from renting physical DVDs and finding ways to keep it profitable. Any profits from online delivery would be in addition to what is shown in Exhibit 1.2.

Problems With Existing Strategy Tools

Given that the problem of managing performance through time is universal, it is astonishing that time charts like those in our exhibits are almost completely absent from business books and management literature. Try looking for yourself next time you find yourself in a business bookstore. So what tools do managers actually use to help them decide what to do?

A regular survey by one of the large strategy consulting firms identifies a long list of management tools (Bain & Company, 2007). However, few of these have won much confidence among managers, with the result that they come and go in popularity like fashions in clothing. The tools fall into several categories:

- simple principles open to wide interpretation, such as vision statements and strategic planning
- substantial changes to business configurations, such as reengineering and outsourcing
- approaches to controlling performance, such as value-based management and the balanced scorecard
- problem-solving methods, such as the five forces, real options, and customer segmentation

A wide-ranging study by another consulting company, McKinsey (Coyne & Subramaniam, 2000), found that there were few strategy tools with sound methodological foundations beyond the industry forces and value-chain approaches set out by Michael Porter in the early 1980s (Porter, 1980). The many qualitative methods available seemed to work well only in the hands of their developers and were limited in their ability to provide robust, fact-based analysis.

To understand the potential value of a sound approach to managing performance through time, it is useful to start by identifying the problems with current approaches to strategy.

SWOT Analysis

Assessing an organization's strengths, weaknesses, opportunities, and threats (SWOT) is a method widely used by managers to evaluate their strategy. Unfortunately, it offers little help in answering the quantitative questions illustrated in Exhibits 1.1 and 1.2. Typically, the concepts are ambiguous, qualitative, and fact-free. Discovering that we have the strength of great products and an opportunity for strong market growth offers us no help whatsoever in deciding what to do, when, and how much to bring about what rate of likely growth in profits.

Opportunities and threats are features of the external environment; as such, they are better dealt with by considering industry forces and political, economic, social, and technological (PEST) analysis (see chapter 4). Strengths and weaknesses, on the other hand, center on the firm itself, so they are related to the resource-based view (RBV) of strategic management.

RBV writers generally devote attention to more intangible resources and the capabilities of organizations on the assumption that tangible factors are easy for competitors to copy and therefore cannot provide the basis for competitive advantage (Barney, 2006; Collis & Montgomery, 1994). Later chapters will show, however, that performance cannot be explained or improved without a strong understanding of how simple resources behave, both alone and in combination, and how they are controlled. Our two examples already illustrate common types of tangible and intangible factors that may need to be taken into account (Table 1.1).

Industry Analysis and Strategy

The analysis of competitive conditions within an industry has dominated efforts to understand and develop firm performance. In summary, this approach says the following:

Table 1.1. Examples of Resources in Alibaba.com and Blockbuster Inc.

Alibaba.com	Blockbuster Inc.
BUYERS	CUSTOMERS
SELLERS	STORES
RANGE OF SERVICES	RANGE OF DVDS
WEB SITE PAGES	FRANCHISEES
REPUTATION AMONG USERS	REPUTATION AMONG CONSUMERS

- We try to make profits by offering products for which customers will pay us more than the products cost us to provide.
- The more powerful our *customers are*, the more they can force us to cut prices, reducing our profitability.
- The more powerful our *suppliers are*, the more they can charge us for the inputs we need, again reducing our profitability.
- If we do manage to make profits, our success will attract the efforts of *competitors, new entrants*, and providers of *substitutes*, who will all try to take business away from us, yet again depressing our profitability.

These five forces—buyers, suppliers, rivals, new entrants, and substitutes—thus explain something of industries' ability to sustain profitability through time.

The impact of Netflix on Blockbuster is a classic example of the five forces at work, made possible by the increasing availability and usage of the Internet. The arrival of Netflix allowed consumers to switch to its lower price service from Blockbuster.

In other markets too, e-businesses can offer valuable products at very low cost by eliminating substantial costs associated with conventional supply chains, resulting in attractive profit margins. Buyers face few switching costs in taking up these alternatives. By getting very big very fast, the new providers establish buying power over their own suppliers and erect barriers against would-be rivals. The established suppliers are the substitutes, whose brick-and-mortar assets weigh them down and prevent them from competing in the new business model.

Unfortunately, the five forces framework also describes quite neatly why most such initiatives are doomed. Buyers who are able to switch to the new offering face very low barriers to switching among the host of hopeful new providers, and do so for the slightest financial incentive. The new business model is often transparent, requiring little investment in assets, so rivals and new entrants can quickly copy the offering. Worst of all, many enterprises see the same opportunity for the same high returns from the same business models, so there is a rush of new entrants. Anticipating hefty future profits, many give away more than the margin they ever expected to make, in the hope that, as the last survivor, they will be able to recapture margin in later years.

We saw the five forces at work again in the fiasco of the subprime lending boom of 2003–2007 that brought the world's banking system to its knees. Someone spotted the opportunity to lend money for home purchases to people whose income levels or credit ratings were low. A fraction of these borrowers would likely default on these mortgages, but that was OK because the much higher interest that was charged to these borrowers would give sufficient income to cover those losses and more.

There was no way to keep this new business opportunity a secret, and nothing about it was hard for bank after bank to copy. New entrants to the market intensified competition, but in this case rivalry took the form not of lower prices but acceptance of increasingly risky customers. Ultimately, the total rate of defaults experienced by the subprime mortgage providers was *not* sufficiently covered by the high interest rates charged, and profitability collapsed. This whole sorry episode was made worse by banks' packaging up of these toxic debts and selling them on to other institutions that did not appreciate the true risk, but fundamentally the whole edifice was built on appallingly bad strategic management.

It Is the Time Path That Matters

At first glance, the industry forces view makes a lot of sense, and there is indeed some tendency for industries with powerful pressure from these five forces to be less profitable than others where the forces are weaker. The implication is somewhat fatalistic: If industry conditions dominate your likely performance, then once you have chosen your industry, your destiny is fixed. However, research has found that industry conditions explain only a small fraction of profitability differences between firms (McGahan & Porter, 1997). It turns out that factors to do with the business itself are far more important drivers of performance.

Management *does* matter: You can be successful in intensely competitive industries or unsuccessful in attractive industries. Moreover, the passive industry forces view takes no account of a firm's ability to create the industry conditions that it wants. In essence, the world is the way it is today because Microsoft, Wal-Mart, Ryanair, and many other firms have made it like this, not because market growth and industry conditions have been handed down from on high.

The competitive forces view places great importance on the concept of barriers that prevent industry participants (the competitors themselves plus customers, suppliers, and others) from entering, switching, exiting, and making other strategic moves. This implies that these barriers are absolute obstacles: If you can clear them, you are "in"; if not, you are "out." But business life is not like that. Many industries include small firms operating quite nicely with only a little of the necessary resources, while larger firms operate from a more substantial resource base. In fact, barriers to entry do not seem like barriers at all; they are more like hills. If you are a little way up these hills, you can participate to some degree, and the further up you are, the more strongly you can compete.

So why are strategy tools so weak at answering the basic question of what is driving performance through time? It turns out that most strategy research is based on analyzing possible explanations for profitability measures, such as return on sales or return on assets. Recently, more sophisticated and appropriate measures have been used, such as returns based on economic profit (profit minus the cost of capital required to deliver that profit). Typically, data are collected for large samples of firms and plausible explanations for performance differences among the sample are tested using statistical regression methods.

Such studies generate an estimate of how much of the variation in the profitability of different firms is explained by the suggested causes. These may be external factors such as competitive intensity, or internal factors such as technology or staff training. Unfortunately, today's profitability ratios are a very poor guide to future earnings and of little interest to investors. Would you, for example, prefer to have $1,000 invested in a firm making 20% margins but with declining revenue or in another firm making 15% but doubling in size every year?

What About Nonbusiness Settings?

The last main criticism that can be leveled against existing strategy methods is that they have little to offer the large number of managers who run organizations that are not primarily concerned with making profits. Public services in many economies have been made quasi-commercial in recent years through privatization, outsourcing, and other structural changes. Nevertheless, substantial fractions of all developed economies are still accounted for by public services. Charities, NGOs, security services, and other organizations also have objectives to pursue and resources with which to pursue them.

Current strategy methods are of little help to such organizations, being almost exclusively built on economic analysis of competitive markets. Yet there is a remarkable similarity between the challenges faced by managers in business and nonbusiness settings (Exhibit 1.3). In all cases, they are expected to have sound answers to three key questions:

1. **Why** is our performance following its current path?
2. **Where** is it going if we carry on as we are?
3. **How** can we design a robust strategy that will radically improve this performance into the future?

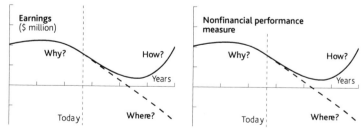

Exhibit 1.3. Performance Questions in Commercial and Noncommercial Settings

Case Example: Ryanair

An example of the failure of conventional industry analysis—and a testament to the success of a resource-based approach pursued over time—is provided by Ryanair. This low-cost airline operates a business model similar to that of Southwest Airlines in the United States. Its success came at a time when the global airline industry faced increased costs combined with static or declining passenger numbers. There was sympathy for the comment from Richard Branson of Virgin that "the safest way to become a millionaire is to start as a billionaire and invest in the airline industry."

Ryanair, like Southwest before it, and easyJet, another budget European operator, challenged the industry situation when it started offering short-haul flights from Ireland's Dublin airport in 1995. The airline focused on creating an ultraefficient operating system, allowing fares way below existing levels in the market and maintaining high levels of customer satisfaction. So dramatic were the low levels of fares that awareness among the public increased rapidly.

Ryanair's success built on the business model originally developed by Southwest, with one type of aircraft (Boeing 737), short-haul travel, no in-flight meals, and rapid turnaround times resulting in air-craft utilization up to 50% greater than the industry average. Ryanair took this approach further, avoiding travel agents, not issuing tickets, selling food and drink on the plane, and building sales through the Internet. These measures developed and reinforced the strategic priorities of efficiency, awareness, and customer satisfaction, and made the airline popular, distinctive, and successful in a fiercely competitive market.

In a sector where intense competitive forces have made the global industry endemically unprofitable for decades, Ryanair, easyJet, Southwest, and a few other determined players have managed to do very nicely indeed.

Diagnosing Performance

A simple example helps to explain how this process of understanding, predicting, and improving performance works in practice. We will start it here and develop it in later chapters.

You find yourself in charge of a restaurant in a medium-size town that gets most of its business from regular customers. You also win a few new customers from time to time, some of whom become regulars. You have had a frustrating time over the past 12 months, as Exhibit 1.4 shows.

As the year started, you were selling 4,000 meals per month and making profits of $18,000 per month. Business and profits increased slowly for a few months, then seemed to reach a limit, so in month 6 you carried out some marketing, hence the decrease in profits and the increase in meals sold. However, meals sold per month soon reached a new limit, so profits also plateaued. In the last months of the year, you cut your marketing spending, saving money and increasing profits sharply, but at the cost of a decrease in meals sold. This kind of account is what we mean by focusing on performance through time: We are not just concerned with static performance measures such as market share, profit margins, or return on capital.

Valuing Performance

A particularly important reason for understanding performance through time is to put a value on firms. Essentially, investors hope to see a strong,

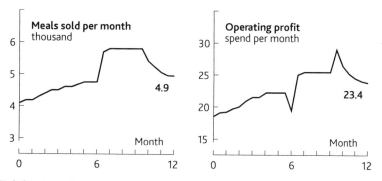

Exhibit 1.4. Restaurant Performance Example

increasing stream of "free cash flow": the cash that is generated after reinvesting what is needed to deliver that growth. Free cash flow is

Operating income + Depreciation – Tax payments + Nonoperating income – Net investments in current assets.

Because investors prefer money sooner rather than later, the forecast free cash flows are discounted back to give a "present value," whether for the firm as a whole or for an investment it intends to make. How these measures are calculated and the method of valuation are explained in detail elsewhere (Copeland, Koller, & Murrin, 2000), so from now on we will simply discuss earnings, profits, or operating income. We will assume that finance professionals can do the necessary translation into the correct financial measures.

The methods used by the finance and investment communities to assess the value of firms and their strategic initiatives are exceedingly rigorous and analytical. Regrettably, though, this rigor is applied to flawed models of how businesses function and speculative estimates of the future. It is during the forecasting stage that financial evaluations lose touch with a firm's strategic reality. A typical approach is to estimate sales growth (on the basis of industry forecasts) and project cost ratios and profit margins (on the basis of assumptions about efficiency improvements). As we will see, there are dynamics at work within organizations that make such approaches to projecting performance highly unreliable.

Action Checklist:
Starting With a Performance Time Path

A sound time path of past and future performance describing the challenge your organization is facing is an essential starting point. It highlights how the future might play out if resources and events continue to develop along their current path. Time paths are not forecasts, and there is little to be gained by trying to get them right. Rather, they describe how the future *could* turn out if things go well or badly.

Time paths provide clarity, helping to shed light on important and complex issues by showing where the current situation may lead and what impact may follow from specific decisions.

Here are some tips for preparing a performance time path:

- Start with a chart of the measure that would ultimately spell success or failure.
- Remember that **numbers matter!** Put a numerical scale and a time scale on the measure you have chosen, going back far enough to cover the explanation for your current situation (except in the case of new ventures, obviously) and far enough into the future to cover the time-horizon of interest.
- In most business-level challenges, a financial outcome is often appropriate, though intermediate outcomes such as sales or customer numbers may work as well, provided the team recognizes that it is assuming these will lead to good financial results.
- In noncommercial settings, adopt the same principle of looking for a performance measure that closely indicates the outcome you are seeking, such as "beneficiaries served."
- Where you are tackling a challenge confined to a single functional area, such as marketing, staffing, or product development, again look for an indicator that will signal progress toward your preferred outcome, such as sales, staff turnover, or product launch rate.
- Use absolute numbers (such as millions of dollars or unit sales) rather than ratios. A 50% return on sales of $10 is not very interesting; nor is an 80% share of a $100 market!
- Consider supporting the main performance chart (e.g., profits, revenue) with a chart of a measure that contributes to that outcome (e.g., unit sales, customers). This can help indicate where you expect the main source of the challenge to lie.

CHAPTER 2

Resources: Vital Drivers of Performance

Overview

Managers already know that building and conserving resources is vital, whether these are tangible items such as staff, cash, and customers, or intangibles such as reputation and investor support. They also understand that resources are interdependent; a firm's winning product range is of little value if poor delivery damages its reputation.

Resources thus represent the crucial foundation. Leadership, capabilities, vision, and all the other subtle and complex concepts we bring to bear can improve performance only if they help us win and retain the necessary resources. This chapter will do the following:

- **explain the link between resources and performance**
- **show you how to identify resources**, keeping the list down to those few simple items that really matter
- **explain how to define and measure resources**, giving you the quantitative understanding you need to manage and use resources successfully

What Makes a Resource Valuable?

The idea that resources are important in business performance goes back more than 40 years but took hold strongly during the 1980s. Today, most strategy books for business students include a chapter on analyzing resources (Grant, 2008). Capabilities and competences are related, but different issues. Think of capabilities as "activities we are good at *doing*," whereas resources are "useful things that we *have*, or can use, even if we don't own them" (Mainardi, Leinwand, & Lauster, 2008; Stalk, Evans, & Shulman, 1992).

Generally, managers focus on the truly *strategic* resources in their business—those few special items that might explain why one firm is more profitable than another. It is widely accepted that resources contribute to sustained competitive advantage only if they score well on most of the following questions (Barney, 2006; Collis & Montgomery, 1994).

- **Is the resource durable**? A resource that quickly deteriorates or becomes obsolete is unlikely to provide sustainable advantage. The *more* durable the resource, the better.
- **Is the resource mobile**? Many resources are so easily moved between firms that they provide little sustainable advantage. People are a clear example. The *less* mobile the resource, the better.
- **Is the resource tradable**? Resources are particularly mobile if they can be bought and sold. The *less* tradable the resource, the better.
- **Is the resource easily copied**? Many resources are easy for competitors to copy, leaving little scope for competitive advantage. The *less* easily copied the resource, the better.
- **Can the resource be substituted by something else**? Even if a resource cannot be bought or copied, an alternative serving the same purpose can erode any advantage. Dell Computers, for example, has negligible presence in retail stores, but its direct supply system is a great substitute. Video conferencing and collaborative working over the Web are substitutes for business air travel. The *less* easily substituted the resource, the better.
- **Is the resource complementary with other resources**? Some resources work well to support one another. The *more* complementary the resource, the better.

Of course, any resource you have that is difficult to copy, buy, substitute, and so on can give you an advantage, but these accepted criteria are neither necessary nor sufficient to explain why one firm beats others.

Consider this situation. You and I run competing restaurants that are next door to each other and identical in almost all respects: same size, same menu, same number of staff with the same experience, and the same likelihood that a passing customer will drop in. The only difference is that you have a million dollars in the bank and I do not.

Now, resources do not get more tradable than cash. I could go and raise a million dollars, but it would cost me more in interest than you will make in interest on your million. It would also take time and effort to obtain, assuming, that is, that I could raise the money at all. What could you do with your million dollars? Develop new products, hire more staff, do more marketing, cut your prices for a while. You have a range of options, any one of which could start winning you more customers and sales than I have. Then you can plough back that extra income to build still more advantage.

Moreover, even if I had one of those supposedly strategic resources, you could *still* beat me. I might have a secret recipe, for example, or exceptionally skilled and loyal staff. All the same, you could quite feasibly overwhelm me simply by spending your extra money on some mundane resources.

This is not just a theoretical game; there are plenty of examples of firms winning with little evidence that they rely on such special resources. Consider McDonald's: Its operating system is crystal clear. Thousands of executives have been through the company and know its operating manuals from cover to cover. Many have used what they learned to start their own fast-food operations. Yet none has come close to overtaking the leader.

Similar observations apply to Southwest Airlines and Ryanair. The day Ryanair started, any one of thousands of airline executives could have set up the same business. There is nothing mysterious about its operating methods. So the only criterion for strategic resources that remains from the list above is, **are your resources "complementary"**? In other words, do they work well together?

Identifying Resources

First, we need to identify resources, and then we need to understand a crucial feature of how they behave. Let us go back to the example of your restaurant and see how we can explain the history of your business performance over the past 12 months, shown in Exhibit 1.4.

Your restaurant is well known in its local market and largely relies on regular customers who on average visit eight times per month. You estimate that you have about 500 regular customers. You have 20 staff in total, each costing you $200 per month for the hours they work. The explanation for your sales and labor costs are therefore as shown in Exhibit 2.1.

"Regular customers" and "Staff" are shown in boxes here because they are two major tangible resources in this business. Your cash and your restaurant's seating capacity are two further resources. These items are critically important because if they do not change, neither does your business performance, provided of course that outside conditions such as competitive prices, the frequency with which customers visit your restaurant, and so on do not change either. If these resource levels *do* change, your profits *must* change immediately.

The first point to note is that **resources are useful items that you own or to which you have reliable access**. "Useful" simply means that they contribute to the rest of the business, either directly by providing sales or indirectly by supporting other items. You do not have to possess a resource for it to be useful. You do not "own" customers or agents, for example, but they are still somewhat reliable: There is a good chance that they will be with you tomorrow.

There is, however, one fundamental feature that customers and staff share, along with all other resources: **The quantity of a resource that you have today is precisely the total of everything you have ever won**

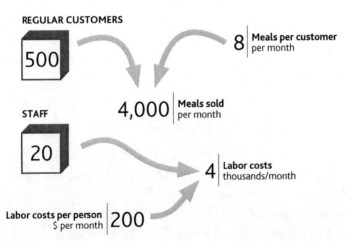

Exhibit 2.1. The Explanation for Restaurant Sales and Labor Costs

minus everything you have ever lost. We will look at the implications of this in the next chapter. But for now we simply need to connect your restaurant's resources to sales and costs to create a complete explanation for your operating profit at the start of the year (Exhibit 2.2).

To understand why customer numbers change through time to create our profit history, we need to learn more about how resources behave. Again, we will cover this in the next chapter.

Defining and Measuring Resources

Resources Involved in Airlines

The case of low-fare airline Ryanair from chapter 1 provides a useful example of business resources and their link to performance. We can take part of the airline's financial history, add data on certain resources, and lay them out in the same graphical form that we used for your restaurant (Exhibit 2.3). Operating profit, on the right of the diagram, comes from revenues minus costs. Revenues result from the number of journeys made by customers and the average revenue from each journey (the fare paid by the passenger plus other items they may buy). "Journeys" do not equate with "customers," however, since customers may travel several times in the course of a year.

Doing It Right: What Our Diagrams Mean

Word-and-arrow diagrams that at first sight look like Exhibits 2.1 and 2.2 are common in business books. Often, though, all they mean is that two items have some general connection.

The diagrams used in this book are different. Every element within them has a specific meaning. The boxes denote resources. The curved arrows indicate that one item can be immediately calculated or estimated from another, as with a formula in a spreadsheet. For example, if you know how many regular customers you have and the frequency with which they buy, you can estimate sales volume; and if you know sales volume and price, you can calculate revenue.

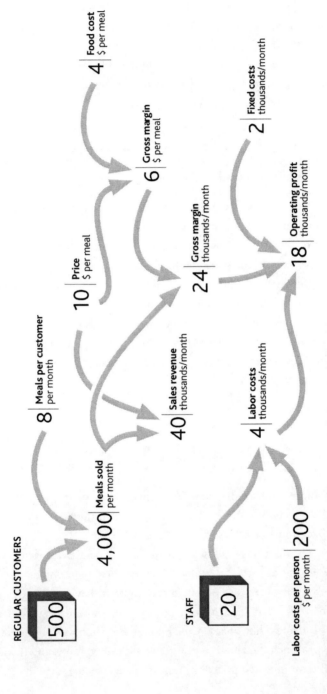

Exhibit 2.2. Your Restaurant's Resources and Operating Profits

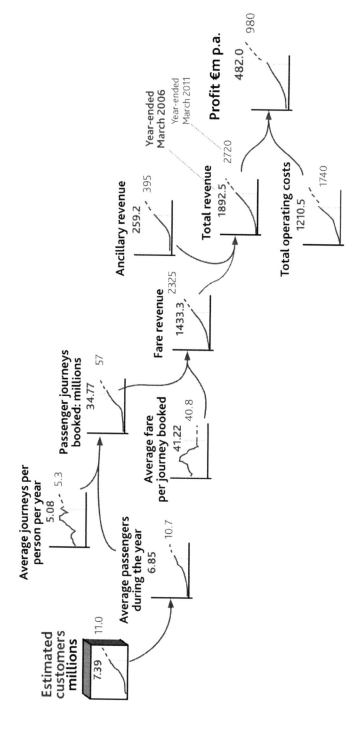

Exhibit 2.3. Explanation of Ryanair's Revenue from 1995 to 2006, and a possible future to 2011

The number of people who travel on Ryanair and the frequency with which they do so are not public knowledge, so we have used indications of plausible historical values. Nevertheless, a number of individuals do travel frequently; others regularly, but less often; and others only occasionally.

Note that, just as customer numbers have driven journeys and revenues up to 2006 (solid lines, bold text values), they will continue to do so into the future, so the exhibit also shows numbers the company might aim for in 2011 (dashed lines and normal text values).

To get the profit number shown on the right of Exhibit 2.3, we also need an explanation for the history and possible future of Ryanair's costs. These are driven by other resources (Exhibit 2.4). Staff numbers drive salaries, aircraft incur fixed operating costs, and there are minimum costs involved in operating each route. An important detail is still missing, however. Costs are not driven only by *having* resources. It is also costly to *win*, *develop*, and *keep* resources. It is costly, for example, to start operations at a new airport, to hire staff, and to acquire aircraft.

Note that this picture of the company's results is not merely a diagrammatic display of the arithmetic of its profit and loss statement. It is a rigorous, *causal* explanation. It therefore provides the start of a sound "theory" of performance. Theory has something of a bad reputation among executives. Believing (correctly!) that management is a practical profession, many see

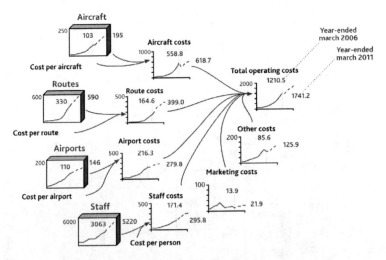

Exhibit 2.4. Explanation of Ryanair's Costs

theoretical concepts as the opposite of what should concern them. They also have good reason to be skeptical about theory, given its patchy record when it comes to providing good advice for organizations. Consequently, few theories are used by management or consulting firms for designing strategy or making strategic decisions. However, executives use some kind of theory every time they make a decision, since they have assumptions about what the consequences will be and why (Christensen & Raynor, 2003). We need to ensure they use *good* theory!

Standard Types of Resource

The airline case features a number of resources shown in the "tanks" on the left of Exhibits 2.3 and 2.4. These four items are examples of some standard and commonly encountered types of resources:

- Passengers are the *customers* that determine demand.
- Airports and routes are effectively the airline's *product range*.
- Aircraft constitute its *capacity*.
- Staff are the *human resources* that operate the whole thing.

Resources often fall into two basic categories: those that drive *demand* for the product (passengers for our airline) and those that are needed to create the *supply* of the product (routes, planes, and staff, in this case).

Demand-Side Resources

The obvious demand-side resource is *customers*. There is one special case in which firms do not have identifiable customers: when they sell into commodity markets such as those for oil, minerals, and agricultural products. For just about everyone else, customers or clients are most important.

However, customers alone may not be all you need to enjoy demand for your product. In many cases you can reach your ultimate customers only through dealers or other *intermediaries*: another demand-side resource. Producers of fast-moving consumer goods (FMCGs) have supermarket companies as their immediate customers, but they ultimately depend on consumers wanting their products. Intel sells processors to computer makers, who sell to stores and resellers, who sell to companies and consumers. All three groups are vital in determining demand for Intel's products.

Demand-driving resources also arise in noncommercial cases. Charities serving the needs of groups suffering disability or homelessness experience demand that reflects the number of people in the group they seek to serve. Nor is demand always a desirable factor: The rate of crime that places demand on police forces reflects the number of criminals.

One thing to be careful about is choosing a performance objective that is itself a resource. For example, DVD rental firm Netflix, whose attack on Blockbuster's stores we discussed in chapter 1, is typical of many firms that feature objectives for customer numbers. Cell phone operators and TV broadcasters also choose to set targets for customer numbers, since they are the key driver of revenues.

Supply-Side Resources

On the supply side, the first resource is the *products and services* that an organization offers in order to satisfy demand. Your restaurant has its menu, a car manufacturer has a range of models, and a law firm has the range of legal services it can provide.

Next, you need some *production capacity* to manufacture or produce your product or service: the capacity of your kitchen to cook meals, or a carmaker's factories and equipment that enable it to manufacture cars at a certain rate.

Doing It Right: Numbers Matter

Although our list of common resource types may be helpful, the fundamental principle in identifying the core resources involved in your specific situation is to work back from the performance you want to explain. This is where sticking to the numbers is so helpful. If you want to explain the "sales" number, you *must*, in most cases, know the number of customers. If you want to explain "labor costs," you *must* know the number of staff, and so on. So start from the chart of performance over time that is bothering you, work back through the way each variable is calculated, and sooner or later you will bump into one or more of these things that fill up and drain away through time.

Making the whole system work requires *people*: Your restaurant's cooks and waiters, a carmaker's production-line workers, and a law firm's lawyers are all resources that enable the organization to function. In certain cases, the production capacity itself may largely be made up of people. The capacity of a law firm, for example, consists of the lawyers who do the work.

Noncommercial organizations have many close parallels to these supply-side resources. Voluntary groups and public utilities offer services and sometimes products to their beneficiaries. Housing charities, health services, and police forces all need capacity to deliver their services. All of these rely on their staffs to deliver their services.

If you are concerned with a functional strategy challenge rather than the overall performance of the organization, chapter 1 mentioned that you will have objectives for indicators relating specifically to that function, such as staff turnover or product launch rate. Here, too, it is possible that you might focus on an objective that is itself a resource. A law firm or an education service, for example, may well have targets to build staff numbers (lawyers or teachers) to certain levels by a certain date.

Financial Resources

We must not forget money! Cash itself is a resource and definitely obeys the rules for resources. The quantity of cash in your bank account today is precisely the sum of all cash ever added to the account minus all cash ever taken out. Debt can be thought of as a "negative" resource.

Action Checklist:
Define and Quantify Resources Driving Performance

From chapter 1, you should have a sound time chart of past and future performance describing the challenge your organization is facing. The next step is to work back along the logical path of factors that account for the values on that chart.

Here are some tips for laying out the link from performance back to the resources that drive it:

- Put your performance time chart to the right of your page.

- Ask what this performance outcome is calculated from (e.g., profit = sales – costs). Put time charts for these items to the left and connect them with arrows to the time chart of the performance outcome (see Exhibit 2.3).
- If you are not focusing on overall financial outcomes as much as some less tangible outcome, such as customer service quality, you may not have such precise arithmetic relationships. Service quality, for example, may depend on "average staff workload." Nevertheless, do try to specify this causal factor precisely in a way that you can quantify.
- Continue asking the question "what causes what" to work back across the page to the left, adding time charts and connections as you go. Stick firmly to the rule that if you know items to the left, you can calculate or estimate the values of items they link to on the right.
- Repeat this until you hit one or more "resource" items. You should not need to make more than two to four links before you hit these items, and you should not find very many of these resources (refer back to examples of typical resources described in this chapter).

Beware of being tempted by relationships that are outside the organization. Sales, for example, are *not* determined by "market size" multiplied by "market share," but by "customers" multiplied by "sales per customer." (Market size is the sum of all companies' sales, and market share is your sales divided by this total.)

If your objective is itself a resource (e.g., to grow the number of customers or staff to some scale by some point in time), there is good news. You do not need to do any of this! You can simply move on to the next step in chapter 3.

CHAPTER 3

Resources and Bathtub Behavior

Overview

Resources have a special characteristic: They fill and drain over time, like water in a bathtub. This chapter explains this behavior, shows why it is so important, and also does the following:

- **explains how to work out what the numbers do** when resources fill and drain
- **shows where management control lies**
- **outlines how managers can develop resources** through time

Bathtubs Rule! Resources Fill and Drain

Since a firm's performance at any time directly reflects the resources available, it is essential that we understand how these resources develop over time and how we can control the process.

Think about the regular customers using your restaurant. These people did not magically come into existence at a particular moment in time; they have *become* loyal customers. Some have been visiting your restaurant for years; others have begun only recently. There will also be people who used to be customers but then stopped. Perhaps they had a bad meal, got tired of the menu, or found another restaurant they preferred.

This idea is captured in Exhibit 3.1. The tank in the middle holds the number of customers you have right now. To the left is the outside world, where there are many people, some of whom may become future

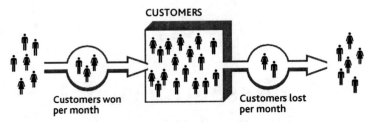

Exhibit 3.1. Building and Losing Customers

customers. The big "pipe" flowing into the tank has a pump that determines the speed at which the tank stock is filling with new customers. On the right, another pump on a pipe flowing out of the tank shows how quickly you are losing customers, and again you can see people in the outside world who include your former customers. Because the tank in this diagram holds the inventory or "stock" of customers, this diagram is known as a stock-and-flow structure.

Let us see how this works. By mailing out discount vouchers to local homes, you hope to pump some new consumers into the tank. However, if you do not have enough staff to provide good service, you will inadvertently increase the speed of the outflow pump and soon lose them again. The number of customers will have filled up, but then drained away again.

After customer numbers have fallen back, your staff should be able to provide good service once more. The outflow pump slows, and your tank

Doing It Right: Focusing on Numbers

The idea of resources filling and draining seems simple enough. After all, we see it happening around us all the time, from the water in our bathtub, to the cash in our bank, to cars in a city, to rabbits in a field. But merely being aware of this process is not enough if we want to take control. We need to know the following:

- **how many** customers, staff, or other resource there are currently
- **how quickly** these numbers are changing
- **how strongly** these factors are being influenced by things under our control and by other forces

returns to a more stable state. The process is a familiar one but difficult to estimate over time.

Exhibit 3.2 shows what would happen to the number of customers in your business if you were to win 50 new people per month but also lose an increasing number of customers every month. You lose 40 people in the first month and an extra 5 people every month thereafter.

The case was made in chapters 1 and 2 that you should always be looking at how things change over time, so these monthly numbers, too, can be shown as time charts. We can still keep the image of the bathtub or tank of customers and the pipes and pumps showing the rate at which customers are flowing in and out of your business (Exhibit 3.3).

The idea that resources fill and drain over time has long been recognized in strategy research (Dierickx & Cool, 1989), so what we will do here is make this mechanism practical to use and connect it to how the rest of the business system works.

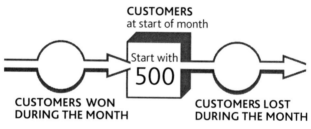

CUSTOMERS
at start of month

Start with
500

**CUSTOMERS WON
DURING THE MONTH**

**CUSTOMERS LOST
DURING THE MONTH**

	CUSTOMERS WON DURING THE MONTH	CUSTOMERS at start of month	CUSTOMERS LOST DURING THE MONTH
January	50	500	40
February	50	510	45
March	50	515	50
April	50	515	55
May	50	510	60
June	50	500	65
July	50	485	70
August	50	465	75
September	50	440	80
October	50	410	85
November	50	375	90
December	50	335	95
End of December		290	

Exhibit 3.2. Working Out Growth and Loss of Customers Through Time

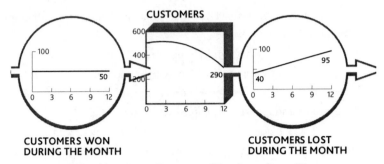

CUSTOMERS WON DURING THE MONTH

CUSTOMERS LOST DURING THE MONTH

Exhibit 3.3. The Change in Customer Numbers Over Time

How Management Control Affects Resources

Why are we so concerned about this "bathtub behavior" that all resources follow? Remember the problem we set out to solve, namely, what determines performance through time and how can management affect performance in the future. The logic is simple:

- The resources in place drive performance at every moment.
- Therefore we must know how the quantity of each resource changes through time.
- These quantities are *only* explained by their inflows and outflows.
- Thus to manage performance through time, the *only* way of exerting control is by managing the flows of resources into and out of the system.

Consider your restaurant and see how these connections work (Exhibit 3.4). In chapter 2 we looked at how the number of meals sold and the operating profits had changed during the previous 12 months and showed how these figures were driven by the number of customers and staff. Following the same logic, we next need to know what happened to customers and staff to bring about the performance history in Exhibit 2.1 *and* the inflows and outflows to these two resources.

It is crucial to explain why the resource of customers developed over time as it did, and the only way to do this is to understand the *flows* (Exhibit 3.5).

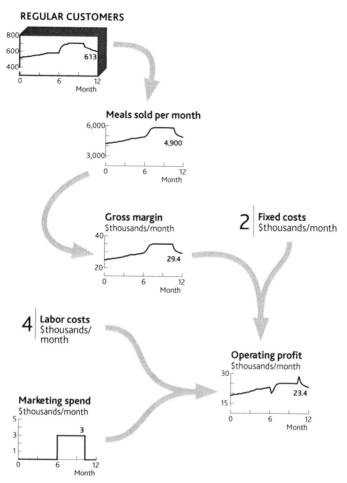

Exhibit 3.4. How Changing Customer Numbers Drives Performance Over Time (for clarity, some items are not shown)

Doing It Right: Units for Resources and Flows

Exhibits 3.2 and 3.3 label the flows entering and leaving the customer resource as "Customers won/lost during the month." This is *always* the relationship between resources and the flows that fill or drain them: Whatever the resource in the tank, the flows are "[resource] per [time period]."

There is never any exception to this rule!

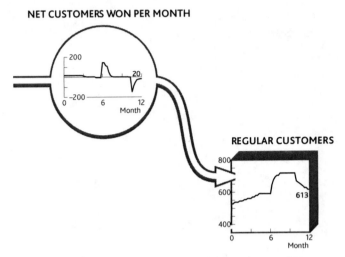

NET CUSTOMERS WON PER MONTH

REGULAR CUSTOMERS

Exhibit 3.5. The Net Flow of Customers Into and Out of Your Regular Customer Group

- It looks as if you had an early small inflow of customers, but this slowed.
- So you did some serious marketing, which brought a flood of customers.
- But this soon died away again, and your customer stock settled down at a steady but higher level, with seemingly no inflow or outflow at all.
- Toward the end of the year, you experienced another flood of customers, but this time it was negative (the downward slope on the customer flow): You were losing customers fast.
- Once again the flood soon slowed to a mere trickle and your stock of customers steadied at a lower level, again apparently with no inflow or outflow.

You can put flesh on these bones. By asking your customers if and when they have previously visited, you get a good idea of the inflow rate. Although you cannot easily ask how many people become *ex*-customers each month (because they are not there to be asked!), you can work out what the outflow must have been to reconcile with the net change each month (Exhibit 3.6).

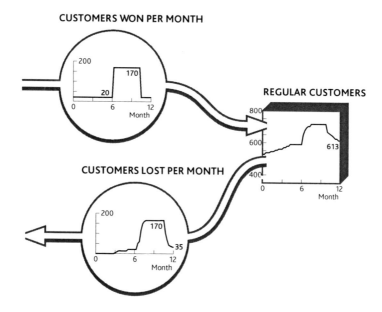

Exhibit 3.6. The Separate Flows of Customers Into and Out of Your Regular Customer Group

Doing It Right: Separating Inflows From Outflows

If your restaurant experienced only the flows shown in Exhibit 3.5, you might be tempted to take the complacent view that nothing much is happening. Apart from the two puzzling spikes of customer gains around month 7 and losses around month 11, everything seems to be ticking along steadily enough.

But appearances are misleading. During the middle period, turbulent activity is taking place, with lots of customers arriving and many others leaving. In fact, customer churn is so rapid that by months 9 and 10, you are almost certainly losing many of the customers that your marketing efforts brought in just a short time before.

The factors driving resource *gains* are typically quite different from those driving *losses*, so you stand little chance of solving these challenges without distinguishing between the two flows.

Always try to identify resource "gain" and "loss" rates separately.

Developing Resources

External Resources

Trying to build resources can be frustrating. For example, take hiring: Suitable staff may be scarce, and you may have to fight your competitors for the limited number of good people. Even if you win that battle or you have no strong competitors, potential staff may be looking at other opportunities that have nothing to do with the market in which you operate. A customer service person at Ryanair could leave to work in a hotel or even to become a teacher, for example.

At least with staff, there may be a continuous stream of new talent coming onto the market. Many other resources are finite. Once everyone has a cell phone, for example, there is no one left to be won and sales efforts have to switch to upgrades and luring people away from rivals. Similarly, chain stores run out of new locations, airlines run out of good routes that passengers may want to fly, and so on.

To capture this phenomenon, we need to be explicit about the stock of *potential* resources as well as the stock of *developed* resources, plus the rate at which we convert one to the other. Exhibit 3.7 shows these elements for a new retail company that has developed a specialty store format and now wants to build outlets in all the towns where it may be successful. On the left are the towns thought to have enough of the right consumers to provide the demand for the stores; there are 100 of these at the outset. On the right is the increasing number of stores operating, and in between is the rate at which stores are being opened.

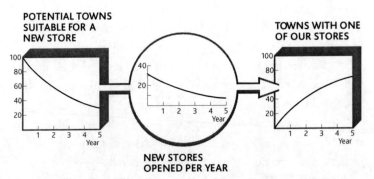

Exhibit 3.7. Developing Potential Locations for a Retail Chain

Understanding how to manage the *development* of resources from a potential pool is vital.

- Identify the scale of *potential* resources—just how many *are* there in the potential pool?
- Assess the rate at which the potential resource can be developed.
- Look for ways to accelerate this development rate.
- Look to stimulate growth of the potential resource itself.

The story of Alibaba.com in chapter 1 is a great example of a company identifying a specific potential resource—the large number of smaller Chinese companies seeking to go global—and developing that potential very rapidly. Once that opportunity was well exploited, it moved on to repeat the trick in other markets.

Resources Within the Business

The challenge of resource development is not confined to the bringing of potential resources into your business system: Certain resources must continue to be developed *within* the organization. The most common of these is staff, though the same challenge also applies to products and customers.

Exhibit 3.8 shows an organization that has become badly out of balance because the flows of people through its internal development chain have been running at the wrong rates. At the most senior levels, promotions appear to be happening slowly, at just six per year. But turnover among senior staff is also low, so the upper ranks have become crowded.

The organization has clearly been promoting experienced staff to senior positions faster than other senior people have been leaving. But things are not quite that simple. Promoting 6 experienced people out of 50 each year, as we were in year 1, meant that experienced people had to wait more than 8 years for promotion. By the time we get to year 5, the wait has grown to 20 years, because of the 100 experienced staff we have, only 5 are promoted each year. So reducing the promotion rate risks leaving experienced staff frustrated and may increase the rate at which

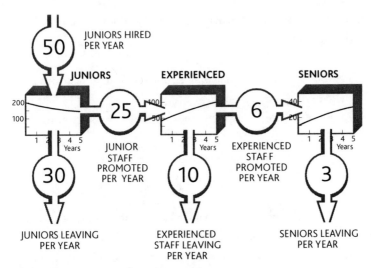

Exhibit 3.8. The Staff Promotion Chain

they leave. Juniors, on the other hand, are not being hired fast enough to replace those who are leaving or are being promoted.

This is why some companies pursue a seemingly perverse staff policy known as "up or out," in which people are expected to seek promotion and are helped to leave if they are not successful. This can apply all the way up to top levels, where retirement or moving on to other organizations is also encouraged. The policy is all about making space for talented people to progress.

Doing It Right: Conserving Resources

Exhibit 3.8 illustrates a further critical principle when resources flow from state to state. The sum of these stocks *must* add up to the total number of staff. They are said to be "mutually exclusive" (i.e., any resource item can appear in *only one* state at any time) and "collectively exhaustive" (i.e., taken together, they account for *all* of this resource in the system)—a principle known as MECE (pronounced "mee-see"). This principle is easily overlooked. It is common, for example, for management to continue talking about a market's total potential even after most of that potential has already been taken up.

The "Choice Chain"

The last extension of this resource development idea concerns an almost universal phenomenon: the development of awareness, understanding, and choice among customers, employees, investors, donors, and other stakeholder groups (Desmet et al., 1998; Finskud, 2009).

We can start by considering a new consumer brand: a soft drink such as Coca-Cola's Powerade sports drink, for example. An individual is unlikely to switch on a single day from complete ignorance of the brand to being a regular and loyal consumer. So we do not simply have a tank of "potential" consumers and a tank of "loyal" consumers; rather, consumers move through a series of stages (Exhibit 3.9):

- Initially, the consumers who we may want will be unaware that our brand exists. The first challenge is to pump them into being *aware*: ensuring that they will have at least heard of the brand, even if it means nothing to them.
- Once they are aware, we need them to *understand* the brand and associate meaning with it—preferably a meaning relating to values that are significant for them.
- When they understand that the brand means something they can relate to, we can hope that they will try the brand, at least on a *disloyal* basis. They may continue purchasing competing brands, but at least we are on their list of options.
- Ideally, we would like consumers to be *loyal* and always choose our brand. This "certain future choice" is rare, but highly valuable if it can be achieved. Coca-Cola itself has attained this status for many consumers, as have brands such as BMW, Wal-Mart, and CNN.

Now, these pumps are expensive to drive. Every advertising and promotional activity costs money, so it is vital to make judicious choices about which ones to drive and how fast, and how to change priorities as time passes. Moreover, while you are trying to do all this, your pool is draining back down the hillside: Consumers are forgetting why your brand is important to them, choosing to buy other brands, or simply

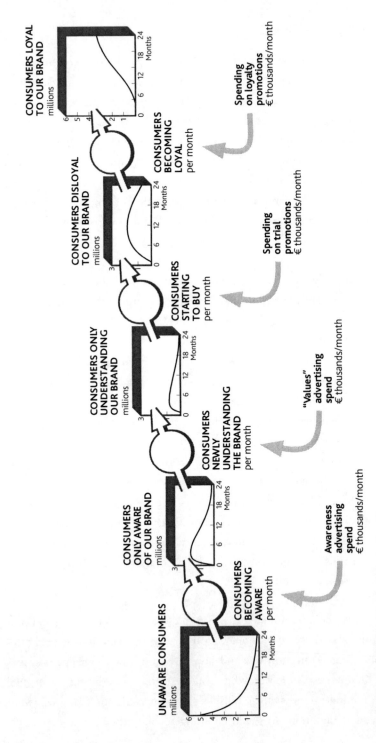

Exhibit 3.9. The Choice Chain for Consumers

forgetting about it altogether, hence the continuing efforts of even the strongest brands to keep reinforcing consumer choice.

In principle, it looks as if you should drive the lower pumps first, then slow them down while speeding up the upper pumps as your pool gets pushed up the hill. But this qualitative approach simply will not do; you need to know *how much* of each activity to do at each moment. Many firms get these choices badly wrong.

One innovative industrial products firm consistently underinvests in all stages of this chain. The only reason it can boast of the high proportion of sales derived from new products is that this underinvestment forces sales managers to switch their effort from older products to the latest novelty. No sooner has the company pumped customers to within reach of becoming loyal then it abandons the effort and they slip back down again into the arms of grateful rivals!

In contrast, the pharmaceutical industry commonly *over*spends on sales. Sales representatives constantly struggle to get to see doctors who already prescribe their product and fully intend to continue doing so. With everyone in the industry making the same futile efforts, it is hardly surprising that one study found only 20% of sales calls in the United States even got to see the doctor and less than half of these calls were remembered (Elling, Fogle, McKhann, & Simon, 2002).

Similar development chains arise for other resources (Sterman, 2000, chap. 12). For some, however, such as product development, you have direct control over how individual items move through the system. Nevertheless, it is still important to know the quantity of resources at each stage and be aware of how your decisions are affecting their development. It is common, for example, for companies to invest effort and cost in developing promising products, only to fail to finalize them and drive them into the market.

Action Checklist: Developing Resources

Work out what is happening over time to the quantity of your resources and what you want to happen in the future. How are the flows of each resource changing? Can you complete a chart like Exhibit 3.3 for your customers, staff, and other critical resources?

Understand the scale of *potential* resources you are developing. In the case of customers, useful questions to ask include the following:

- *How many* potential customers are there?
- Does this scarcity impose any constraints on the *rate* at which you can develop customers in future?
- Is anything happening to the potential customer pool itself? For example, are your efforts and those of competitors filling up the tank of potential customers, even while others are being converted to active customers?

For any groups whose "choice" you have to win, you can usefully ask the following:

- What exactly defines this overall population? Who are they, and how many of them are there in total?
- Again, what distinct *stages* do they move through?
- How many are in each stage, and at what rate are they moving up and down the chain?
- Do the numbers add up? Everyone in your defined group should be in one stage, and one stage *only*, at any moment.
- Is anything happening to the group overall? Are demographic changes bringing new potential customers into existence?
- And, of course, what are you doing, to what extent, that influences these flows, and by how much?

CHAPTER 4

Driving the Machine: Handling Interdependence Between Resources

Overview

The way that resources increase or decrease through time is critical, and resources always rely on one another. Existing resources either enable growth in other resources or constrain it. This mutual reliance can even lead the whole system to collapse.

The next step is to show how these mechanisms make resources complementary and explore the implications of this interdependence over time. This chapter will do the following:

- **show how resources can drive their own growth**
- **explain how growing a resource depends on the availability of other resources**, creating self-reinforcing feedback that can drive rapid growth or lead to collapse
- **describe how having too little of one resource can constrain another's growth** but also protect against decline
- **highlight the impact of these interdependences on performance through time**

Gaining and Maintaining Resources

So far we have learned the following:

- Understanding and managing performance through time is the key challenge for management (chapter 1).

- Performance depends on resources: items that fill and drain (chapter 2).
- The way that resources flow into and out of the organization, and from stage to stage, is critically important and difficult to manage (chapter 3).

The next crucial question is, **what drives the growth (inflow) and decline (outflow) of resources**?

There are three factors moving resources into and out of your organization:

1. **Your own decisions**, for example, marketing spending, sales effort, firing staff, and research and development (R&D) efforts
2. **Outside forces**, for example, changes in customers' needs, shortages of suitable staff, price cuts by competitors, and increases in expected service levels
3. **Resources already in place**, for example, salespeople to win customers, service people to deliver service and retain clients, and research staff to develop new products.

Decisions Affect Resource Flows

In fact, most of your own decisions—at least those that are likely to affect performance into the future—work by affecting resource *flows*, either directly or indirectly. You recruit more salespeople to win customers faster, add service capacity to keep customers from leaving, take on engineers to develop products, dedicate human resource (HR) staff to hiring, and so on.

If we start training people today, for example, we do not *instantly* get better bottom-line performance. The training improves the overall skill of the group over whatever time it takes to cover everyone in the group. Only those people who have been trained can start to deliver improvements, and this takes time. The one impact we do see immediately, of course, is the extra cost! Consequently, it is all too common for organizations to decide on beneficial changes, only to abandon them because they do not see enough immediate benefit to continue. What often gets cut first when performance falters? Training and marketing!

Let us look back at what happened to your restaurant over the past 12 months. Exhibit 3.6 showed the inflow and outflow of regular customers.

The decisions involved were to increase marketing spending but then cut back later in the year (Exhibit 4.1).

Note that we are not looking to explain the impact of marketing on profits, not even on sales. The *immediate* effect is on the customer win rate, and we need to focus on the numbers: the *rate* of marketing spending and *how much* impact it had on the rate of winning new customers. It also seems that our marketing decisions are not quite enough to account for the customer win rate, since we had a trickle of new customers even when we were spending nothing.

We must not forget that such a change in a resource flow is not the only consequence of our decisions. Many will have cost or revenue implications, too. In this case, marketing spending has an *immediate* impact on profits, as well as causing other changes (Exhibit 4.2).

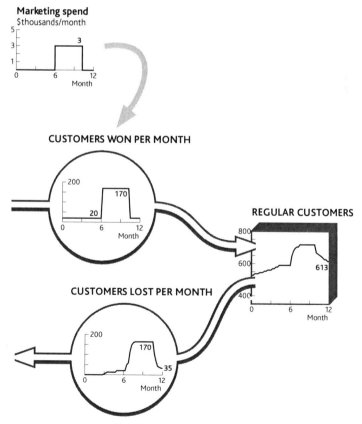

Exhibit 4.1. Marketing Decisions Change the Inflow of Customers

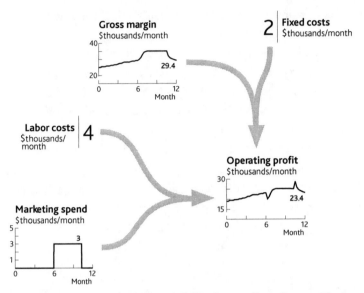

Exhibit 4.2. The Impact of Changed Marketing Spending on Profits

When you increased spending in month 7, profits dropped by the amount you decided to spend. Profits grew quickly after you implemented this decision, so something else must have happened. But the *immediate* effect was a sharp drop: no delays or bathtubs filling in this part of the system, just simple arithmetic. The same applies to the decision in month 10 to *cut* marketing spending. The profit rate *immediately* jumps by the $3,000 per month cut in marketing. Again, however, something else happens soon after to wipe out that profit increase.

Outside Forces Affect Resource Flows

Competitors and other factors also affect the flows of resources into and out of our business. Competitors can even *help* us develop resources, as we will see in chapter 7. External influences are generally looked at under four categories:

1. **Political** changes, such as privatization and deregulation, open up entire industries. Some may even act directly on specific aspects of performance, such as price regulation in utility markets.

Doing It Right: Stick to the Correct Language

We are often sloppy in our use of language about business, and since we have never been especially conscious of the bathtub behavior of resources there is a particular problem about *levels* and *rates*. We might discuss what we can do to increase the "level" of profits, say, or debate whether the "level" of marketing spending is sustainable. Wrong! Profits and marketing spending are both *rates* at which money is being made or spent; their units are dollars *per month*. The only factors that should properly be referred to as "levels" are resources, plus that rather special factor, price.

This may seem picky, but so long as we are inaccurate in the language we use, we will continue to misunderstand what is going on. And if we misunderstand, we will misdecide!

2. **Economic** changes constantly bring new customer groups into existence. Fast-developing economies can create conditions in which the inflow to the "potential customer" pool grows extremely rapidly. The opposite occurs when economies contract, as many companies experienced with the banking-led recession of 2008.

3. **Social** changes drive the migration of consumers, employees, and others into and out of the resource base of different industries. Simple demographic changes bring new young consumers into a potential market each year and of course take them out again as they age.

4. **Technological** progress largely manifests itself in two ways: changing the functionality of products and reducing the unit cost of offering them. Growing Internet penetration helped Alibaba.com but hurt Blockbuster Inc. in our examples from chapter 1.

The systematic examination of these forces is known as PEST analysis. While the concept of PEST influences sounds right, that is not sufficient for strategy development. Once again, numbers matter. You need to understand the *scale* and *timing* of the changes affecting your future. Imagine you run a company producing electronic goods, and you face an economic downturn. You need to know roughly how severe it will be, at what rate it will remove potential consumers from your pool of resources, and to what level.

In addition, factors changing *other* markets can have powerful spin-off effects. TV viewing has fallen as viewers switched their time to online activities, with damaging consequences for advertising revenues. Internet usage in Europe has in turn been depleted by the time people spend sending text messages by mobile phone. These are both examples of quantifiable dynamics—that is, rates of change through time—concerning the influence of substitute products that feature in standard industry forces approaches to strategy (see chapter 1).

Resources Determine Each Other's Growth

The most important point about what drives resource flows, however, is that current levels of resources determine the rate at which other resources fill up or drain away. This is the mechanism for which the system dynamics method is ideally suited (Sterman, 2000, chap. 8).

This is the reality of how resources work together, creating a system that can either perform strongly or constrain its own development. Interdependence can even bring about an organization's self-destruction. Since we know that performance depends on resources, and that only flows of resource can alter these quantities through time, it follows that the *only* means by which management decisions can change your resources through time is by influencing what happens to the inflows and outflows.

However, as chapter 2 highlighted, you cannot build any resource without using resources already in place. This interdependence has two implications:

1. The more of a resource you *currently* have, the faster others can grow. (It is even possible for a resource to generate its own growth, as when, for example, customers recommend their friends become customers.)
2. Conversely, having too little of a resource right now can slow or stop the growth of other resources. If this shortage is too severe, it can even cause other resources to be lost, which is where self-destruction can arise.

There are many examples of this principle:

- The more salespeople you have, the faster you can win new customers.
- The more development engineers you have, the faster you can improve the range and quality of your products.
- The more donors a charity has, the faster it can acquire the cash it needs.
- The more good clients a professional firm has, the faster it can win the best staff.

In the cases listed above, if you had none of the first resource, the second would not grow at all unless some *other* resource could replace it. If you have no salespeople, for example, you will need agents, a Web site, or some other alternative to capture customers. If a charity has no donors, it will need government funding or some kind of endowment to carry on its work.

So how does a new business ever get started? It turns out that entrepreneurs too must have *some* stock of experience, contacts, and personal credibility to allow them to raise cash and hire their first staff. (Experience and credibility are intangible resources, which we will look at in chapter 8.)

Reinforcing Feedback

Resources Can Stimulate Their Own Growth

The simplest case of mutual support is when a resource drives *its own* growth. This process can be seen in an everyday situation: cash and interest. The more cash you have saved, the faster more cash is added to it. Another obvious case is word of mouth among consumers. Our basic principle of reinforcing feedback still applies: The *more* consumers there are, the *faster* they can win new ones (provided, that is, there are plenty of potential consumers left to be won).

This is much more than a qualitative notion; as we keep emphasizing, *numbers matter* and can be worked out. Exhibit 4.3 takes us back to the start of chapter 2 and the simple customer stock at your restaurant. Let us imagine this time, however, that there is no loss of customers at all. In fact, you are winning more, thanks to the positive word of mouth from your existing clientele. Every 10 customers you have leads to you winning 1 new customer every month. Starting with 500, you win 50 during January. February then starts with 550, so that month you win 55, and so on.

You can see just how powerful reinforcing growth can be. By the end of the year the business is growing at almost three times the rate it was at the start. This may seem an astonishing and unrealistic rate of development, but it is very common indeed—look back at Alibaba.com in chapter 1, or think how quickly Skype took off. The reason it seems unusual is that we do not often experience it ourselves, and other organizations we see around us may be too small to be noticed while the process is in full swing.

It seems, though, that apart from cash and people-based resources, there are few other examples that are capable of this self-replicating behavior. This is because most other resources are inanimate and just sit there unless we do something with them. So we need to turn our attention now to the way one resource drives growth in others.

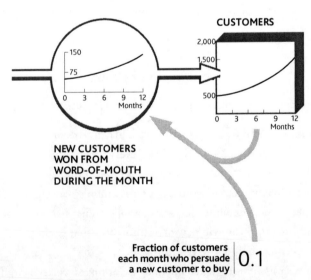

Exhibit 4.3. The Arithmetic of Reinforcing Growth From Word of Mouth

How Existing Resources Drive Growth in Others

Consider the example of the consumer brand introduced in chapter 3. Building awareness and interest in a brand is essential, but if we actually want to *sell* anything, we have to get stores to stock it. A new brand thus needs to drive the *inflow* to the resource of stores stocking the brand. What other resources are required to achieve this?

First, we need consumers who want to buy the product. Retailers will not stock a product that is unlikely to generate profits for their stores, and these profits will only arise if consumers are likely to buy. A stock of interested consumers is not enough. Retailers need to know about the product and its potential profitability and must be constantly reminded of its attractiveness relative to other uses they might have for their shelf space. This requires a sales force. In this case, then, *two* resources are required: consumers and a sales force. If either is missing, stores will not be won. Exhibit 4.4 shows how these two resources drive growth in stores.

This may seem a daunting mix of numbers to get your head around, so let us think through how a product manager might estimate these numbers, based on either experience with previous brands or from seeing what competitors have accomplished.

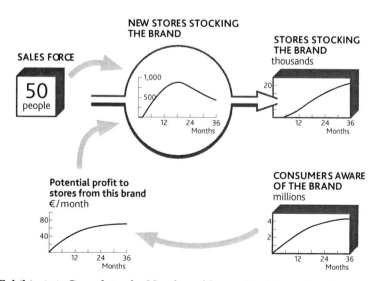

Exhibit 4.4. Growth in the Number of Stores Stocking a Brand Depends on Sales Force and Consumers

Our 50 salespeople can each make about 100 calls per month; that is 5,000 calls per month in total. However, it takes several calls to persuade a store that the brand is attractive, so perhaps only one call in four might be expected to achieve a sale. At first, so few consumers want the product that stores do not see much profit to be made, so sales calls are not successful at all. As consumer demand grows, the rate of sales success climbs.

Later, stores are won increasingly slowly because we are running out of stores to win. Exhibit 4.4 is therefore incomplete; we need to see the falling stock of potential stores as well, as shown in Exhibit 4.5.

Running out of potential stores is not the only reason for the limited win rate, however. The product manager needs to go through a few steps in order to estimate this win rate over the 2 years of the product launch (Exhibit 4.6).

- The *horizontal solid line* shows the maximum that could be achieved if all sales calls contributed to winning stores and every store found the product sufficiently profitable to stock.
- The *solid curve* grows toward the maximum store win rate as our advertising gradually reaches the consumers whose demand makes the product desirable to stores.
- Unfortunately, by the time we get close to this maximum rate,

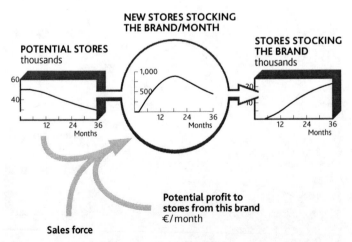

Exhibit 4.5. Limited Potential Slows Growth in Stores Stocking the Brand

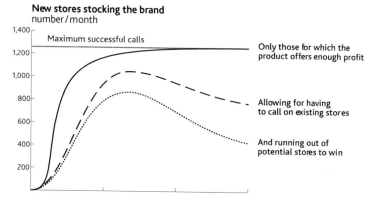

Exhibit 4.6. *Estimating Sales Force Success Over Time*

our salespeople are busy looking after existing stores (*dashed line*).

- Finally, as the remaining potential stores become scarcer, the win rate is reduced still further (*dotted line*).

The product manager can use the same process to estimate how rapidly consumers might be made aware of the brand. Two factors drive awareness: the firm's own advertising expenditures and the brand's presence in stores.

We now have some circularity in our reasoning. Growth in consumer awareness depends in part on the resource of stores, and growth in stores depends on the number of consumers. Putting these two together gives

Doing It Right: Using Connecting Arrows

As we have emphasized before, the connecting arrows in these diagrams mean much more than some vague relationship between one item and another. They mean that you can estimate the value of an item at any time if you know the values of all the factors linked into it with arrows. Adding the arrow from "Potential stores" to "New stores stocking the brand/month" in Exhibit 4.5 is therefore critical: You cannot estimate the rate of new stores without knowing the potential.

us a precise picture of what we mean when we say that our resources are complementary.

Finding the Drivers of Resource Flow Rates

In the case of winning stores for a brand, it is relatively easy to identify and confirm the main factors in the win rate: namely, stores that will profit from the brand, the number of salespeople, and available stores. The explanations are not always so clear, however, so you will need to discuss with colleagues the factors most likely to drive a flow.

Imagine that staff turnover is causing you concern. There may be many reasons for this. How have your salaries changed, as well as those offered by your competitors? Has there been a change in the number of other job opportunities? Have competitors been increasing their hiring efforts? Has there been a change in your employees' workload?

It is possible that by putting the history charts for these items around the flow you want to explain (staff lost per month), you will easily see what has been happening and why. However, it may be necessary to go further. One place to start is to ask people why they chose to act as they did. In this case, exit interviews will provide some information on why staff turnover is happening.

It may be that you will need to use statistical methods to see if your expected drivers really do explain the resource flow rate. **Beware!** The accumulating behavior of resources makes it unsafe to use correlation to explain resource levels. Remember that today's customers are precisely the sum of all you have ever won minus all you have ever lost, so no *other* causal explanation can be meaningful, however good the correlation may seem to be.

However, you *can* safely use correlation to confirm possible causes of resource flow rates. One retail bank found an astonishingly close relationship between certain factors and the rate at which any branch was likely to see customers closing their accounts. Among these strong causes was the bank's history of making mistakes with customers' accounts.

Limits and Pitfalls With Reinforcing Feedback

As long as the growth rate continues, this self-reinforcing mechanism generates positive expansion. In the absence of any constraints, this growth will be exponential, increasing by the same *proportion* in each period. This is clearly a favorable situation for any firm to create, but there are three precautions to note:

Reinforcing growth is not free. Something has to create the resource in the first place. In our brand example, this kick start came from the advertising, without which nothing would have happened. Salespeople can only persuade stores to stock the brand if consumers are interested. In practice, salespeople might conceivably persuade stores to take a product on the promise that consumers *will* become interested, even if they are not yet. But this relies on the reputation and credibility of the sales force—another intangible resource that has to be built. There is no free lunch!

Reinforcing growth cannot continue indefinitely. Growth will inevitably come up against limits, either external (no more customers to win) or internal (not enough capacity to supply new customers). Even apparently unstoppable firms like McDonald's and Coca-Cola hit the limit at some point, although that limit can be very high indeed.

Reinforcing feedback is capable of driving collapse. This problem arises when a decline in one resource leads to another resource draining away. This may in turn mean lower marketing spending, more people leaving the business to go to competitors, damage to the firm's reputation, and possibly other related problems. In essence, the difficulties facing the business escalate and reinforce each other.

How Interdependence Causes Collapse

Organizations that rely on professional staff run the risk of self-reinforcing collapse. Examples arise in both businesses and public services: lawyers in a legal firm, information technology (IT) department staff, hospital nurses, police officers, and so on. Collapse happens through a sequence of events. Staff can initially cope with the demands made on them while their workload remains constant. However, this group gradually depletes through normal staff turnover. As numbers decline, the pressure on those who remain increases, leading to further turnover and yet more pressure.

In such cases, the system needs at least a temporary reprieve from the pressure to arrest the loss of staff. This can come from two principal sources: using temporary staff such as contractors, or reducing the workload, either by turning work away or simplifying what is done. These fixes come with their own dangers. Contract staff can actually make matters worse by needing guidance from the already pressured staff and by further demoralizing them. Turning work away may be advisable, but it can be an uphill struggle to persuade managers to do this when they are already facing business collapse.

Work pressure is not the only trigger for collapse. One consulting firm serving the finance industry lost just a few key clients. With less rewarding projects to work on, and with their professional reputation to worry about, key staff resigned and moved to competing firms. This loss of key consultants caused still faster loss of clients, some of whom actually moved with the consultants to the same competitor! And so the process continued until the firm effectively collapsed.

Critical to solving this problem is to decide quickly *what to do, when, and how much*. Diagrams like those in Exhibits 4.4 and 4.5 clarify the problem and shed light on the path out of trouble. They also provide a map of progress as the solution develops.

It is better, of course, to have a plan for solving these troubles *before* they ever arise. But best of all is to have a mutually supporting set of resources whose interdependence is so positively embedded that the risk of a complete collapse is always remote.

Checking for Reinforcing Feedback

To see if your situation will reinforce growth or decline among one or more of your resources, the question to ask is, **If this resource grows (or declines), will it have consequences that lead to further growth (or decline)**?

We know these mechanisms as virtuous or vicious cycles. To find out, sketch the resources, flows, and intervening factors, and work through the story.

Exhibit 4.7 tells the story for our consumer brand. Starting at the bottom left, if the number of consumers increases, the potential profit available to stores increases, causing more to stock the product. As it becomes more visible, additional consumers are won more quickly. However, do not forget the self-limiting effect that comes from running out of both resources.

How Growth Is Constrained

We now return to the other class of interdependence between resources, where an inadequate quantity of one resource slows and stops the growth of others. We can illustrate this by returning to the example of your restaurant.

Exhibit 3.4 showed a slowdown in customer growth, which even your strong marketing efforts failed to increase for more than a short time. Exhibit 3.6 explained separately the inflows and outflows that led to this. The questions we are left with are (a) Why did your customer growth stall in the early months? and (b) Why did customers leave in such high numbers from August through November? The clue lies in what happened to staff numbers during the year: nothing! You had 20 staff members throughout.

Customer numbers were fairly stable until you did your big marketing push, although by June you were losing nearly as many customers each

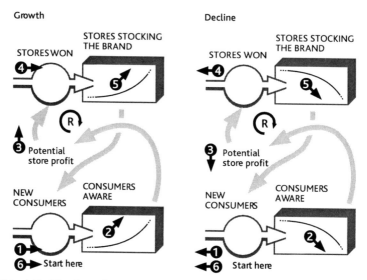

Exhibit 4.7. Checking for Self-Reinforcing Growth and Decline Among Interdependent Resources

month as you were gaining. It seems that your staff were at the limit of their ability to cope. This is borne out by the information on customer service quality shown in Exhibit 4.8. When service quality was high, customer losses were low, but when service quality took a dive, customer losses shot up.

Data on service quality, by the way, are not hard to estimate, even if you do not research them scientifically. Staff tips, complaints, and customer comment cards all offer simple information from which to estimate service quality. The resulting numbers may not be precise, but they are good enough to explain what's happening and guide corrective action.

So now we can pursue the causal linkages and ask *why* service quality suffered. It seems your staff could only cope with the 4,000 meals per month bought by your original 500 customers. When sales jumped to well over 5,500 per month thanks to your marketing efforts, service quality dropped sharply: Your resources were badly out of balance.

If we connect parts of Exhibit 3.5 with Exhibit 4.8, we can see how this story played out (Exhibit 4.9) and explain what happened to your restaurant over the past year.

- Early on, a small number of new customers were arriving in your restaurant every month.
- By the middle of the year, service quality had dropped a little— just enough to put some customers off (the small outflow rate shown in months 4 to 6).

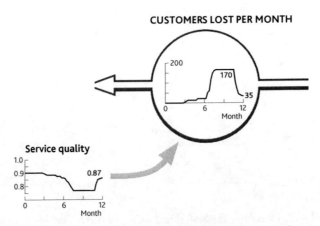

Exhibit 4.8. The History of Service Quality and Customer Losses

- Your marketing campaign in July brought in a rapid flow of new customers: up to 170 per month.
- But your staff could not cope, and customers started leaving more rapidly.
- In a short time, customer losses caused by poor service matched the fast rate of customers brought in by your marketing.
- When you gave up the marketing effort, customer losses continued until they reached a level that where your staff could cope.

There are always limits to how far this cycle of reinforcing growth can go. Balancing mechanisms set in at some point: either you run out of

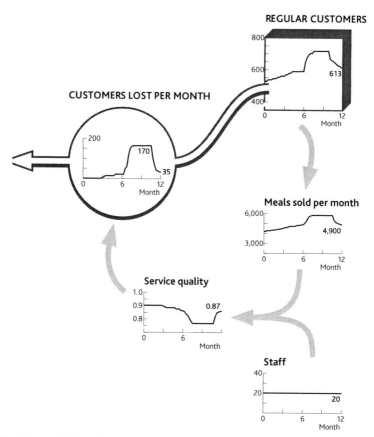

Exhibit 4.9. Why Service Quality Suffered Then Recovered

potential resource or you run up against constraints caused by finite levels of *other* resources. Such balancing feedback structures can also be discovered by tracing back what is causing any resource flow to run at the rate it is. Detecting and managing these balancing effects can remove brakes on growth and protect organizations against overshoot or runaway collapse.

Action Checklist:
Understanding and Leveraging Interdependence

Here are some tips for analyzing the interdependence between resources and using your resulting understanding to manage their development:

- Start with a chart of the history of a resource whose growth you want to understand and control.
- Identify, separately, the history of its inflows and outflows. You may have to do some investigation and reasoning. If, for example, you know your historic staff numbers, the change from month to month is the *net* inflow. You may not know the loss rate. However, you *may* know the hiring rate; in which case the loss rate is the difference between this hiring history and the history of net staff changes.
- The key variables you now want to explain are these separate inflows and outflows.
- Discuss the most likely factors driving a flow and find or estimate how these have changed over the same history. How many new staff did you *try* to hire month by month, and how many did you succeed in hiring? (Target hiring is clearly likely to influence actual hiring!) How have you changed starting salaries, for example, and how have your competitors' starting salaries moved?

It is possible that putting the history charts for these items around the flow you want to explain will clarify sufficiently what has been happening and why. But it may be necessary to go further:

- Use statistical methods to see if your proposed explanations actually explain the resource flow rate.
- If your initial list of causes does not seem to explain how resource flows have changed, go back and investigate what might be missing.
- When you are reasonably confident in your explanations for the resource flow you want to manage, work back to explanations for each of these factors in turn. Staff pressure, for example, will reflect total workloads divided by staff available.

Eventually, you will get back to *existing* resources, and you will have completed the chain of interdependence. Staff turnover will perhaps be explained by current number of customers (driving workload) and existing number of staff. You can now work around all these explanations for the resource flow with your colleagues and assess the likely effectiveness of any options that may be available to manage that flow into the future.

CHAPTER 5

Building and Managing the Strategic Architecture

Overview

We now have everything we need to develop and use a complete picture of your organization's performance. This chapter will show you the following:

- **how to assemble a complete strategic architecture of your business** involving performance, resources, flows, and interdependences
- **how to use this architecture** to manage the system, understanding past performance, likely developments, and alternative possibilities
- **how to control performance into the future**

Remember the strategy challenges that we highlighted in chapter 1? These were

- *Why* has performance followed the path that it has?
- *Where* is it going if we carry on as we are?
- *How* can we change it for the better?

Now that you understand the way a system of resources works, you are in a position to answer these questions in detail.

Building the Strategic Architecture

Why Has Performance Followed a Particular Path?

Earlier chapters have given us all the elements we need to develop a complete picture of our business, together with the information that explains why it has performed as it has up to now. These pieces are as follows:

- **the time chart of one or more performance measures** (e.g., profits, sales, service levels), with scale and timing
- **the list of likely resources involved** (e.g., customers, clients, staff, products, services, cash, capacity)
- **the chain of immediate causes for that performance**, often with simple arithmetical relationships (e.g., gross margin, revenue, labor costs, customer demand)
- at the head of those causal chains, **the resources driving demand, supply, and performance** (e.g., customers, staff, products, services, cash)
- **the flows of resource** (e.g., customers won and lost per month; staff hired, promoted, or leaving per month; products added or discontinued per year) into, through, and out of the organization's system
- **the immediate causes of these rates of flow**, whether your own decisions or other factors
- **the dependence of each resource flow on existing resources**, either for the same resource or others

To illustrate these stages, let us go back to the performance of your restaurant that you wanted to understand before deciding what to do next. Start by pulling the pieces together.

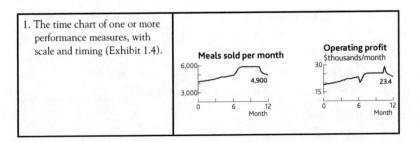

1. The time chart of one or more performance measures, with scale and timing (Exhibit 1.4).

Meals sold per month
6,000
3,000
4,900
0   6   12
Month

Operating profit
$thousands/month
30
15
23.4
0   6   12
Month

2. The list of likely resources involved. (Note: Not all of these may be needed to tackle a specific challenge. Subsequent stages will identify those that *are* involved.)	
3. The immediate causes of that performance (Exhibit 2.1).	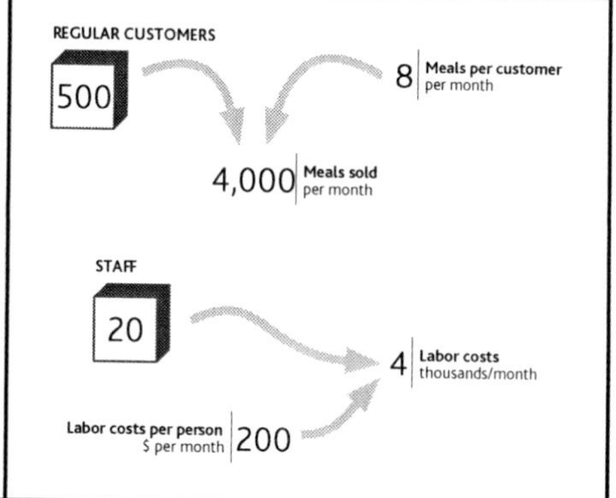
4. The resources driving demand, supply, and performance (Exhibit 2.2).	

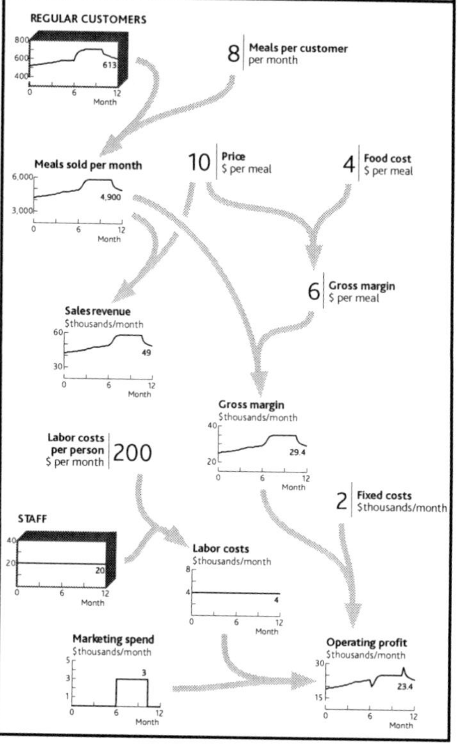

Resource / **Measure**

Regular customers — People
Staff — People
Menu — Items
Capacity — Seats
Cash — $

5. The flows of resources into, through, and out of the organization's system (Exhibit 3.6).	
6. The immediate causes for these flows to be running at the rate they are (a) why customers are being won (Exhibit 4.1 shows the "normal" rate at which new customers arrive, plus those won from your marketing spending). (b) why customers are being lost (extended version of Exhibit 4.8).	
7. The dependence of each flow on *existing* resource levels (Exhibit 4.9).	

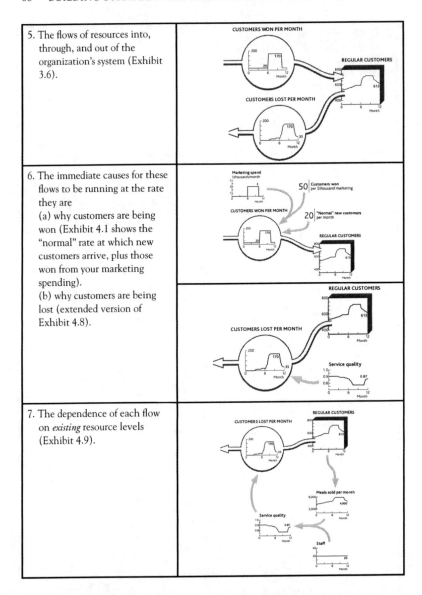

Doing It Right: Do Not Try to Do Everything

Exhibit 5.1 is far from a *complete* architecture of your restaurant. It does not, for example, include certain resources, such as the menu or the seating capacity. Nor does it include potentially important factors that could drive changes in performance, such as price or competitors' actions. The best approach is to include as much of the architecture as is necessary to create a plausible explanation of performance over time.

This needs great care!

- First, do not do unnecessary work, such as collecting data on things that are not relevant. Keep the pictures to a minimum, so you can show people what is happening and why.
- Conversely, check you do not leave out factors that are (or could be) important. This is especially tricky when looking forward rather than just trying to explain the past.
- Finally, when you have an architecture that explains performance, ask whether you have missed anything that may be important to the question you set out to answer.

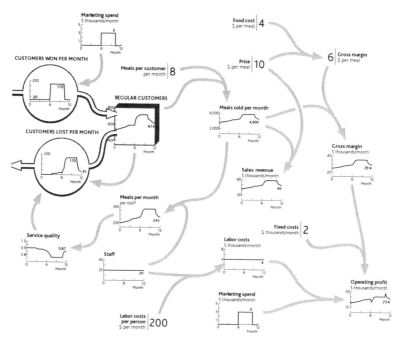

Exhibit 5.1. The Strategic Architecture of Your Restaurant, With Data Explaining Recent Performance

These elements connect together to provide a complete explanation of recent performance and future challenges (Exhibit 5.1).

Using the Architecture

How Have We Come to This Position?

A strategic architecture provides a living reference for a firm's structure and behavior. A critical part of top management's job is to understand that structure, ensure that it is well designed, and steer its performance (Keough & Doman, 1992). Diagrams such as Exhibit 5.1 are a common way of understanding and controlling complex systems. Even if you have never visited a chemicals plant or power station, flown an aircraft, or managed a rail network, you will have seen pictures of "control panels" that give management continuous information on the states of key variables. Their control panels *look like* the system they are managing.

We are trying to achieve the same analog-style diagram for your organization. To make best use of such a picture, you need to have it available and accessible to your whole team, perhaps on a large wallboard in the main meeting room. It may be helpful to have other diagrams in other meeting rooms to show more detail about the architecture of key parts of the system: a diagram of customer segment details in the marketing area, a diagram of people flows in the human resource (HR) department, and so on.

You may not get it right the first time. However, any inaccuracies will become apparent as you learn whether the relationships you have sketched between the connected data provide a good explanation of what is happening. If not, you can readily identify what may be missing or inaccurate and revise the architecture diagram accordingly.

A well-developed strategic architecture is a powerful tool, both to resolve specific issues and to guide the performance of the entire enterprise strategy. To understand this, consider a rather more extensive example than your restaurant: the architecture of a low-fare airline (similar to Ryanair, which is featured in chapter 2). Exhibit 5.2 shows the first 2 years of operation, followed by a possible 3-year future, denoted by the dotted portion of the lines.

It looks complicated, but if you take it in sections, you can see how the stages come together:

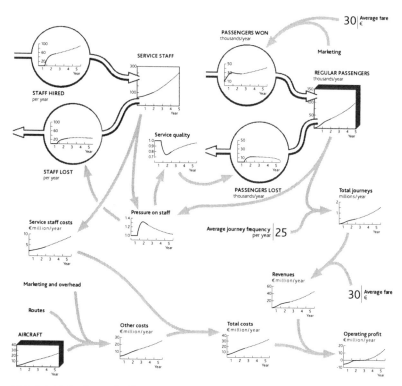

Exhibit 5.2. Growth Slowdown for a Low-Fare Airline

Doing It Right: Whole Numbers

The chart for aircraft in this example shows a smooth line, even though this resource comes in batches; operating 7.5 planes, as it seems you did at one point in year 2, does not make sense. Strictly, we should have a stepped chart over time for aircraft, with a jump to a new number each time a batch of ordered aircraft is received. But for a strategic view of what is happening you do not need to worry about this picky detail.

- Issues of concern by the end of year 2 are operating profit (bottom right), which seems to have stalled, and total journeys (middle right), where growth has slowed.
- The core resources are aircraft, passengers, and staff (routes, too, but we can add these later).
- The immediate factors driving operating profits can be traced back through revenues to total journeys, and through total costs to staff and other cost drivers (in practice, these would be split further).
- The flows of resources into, through, and out of the organization's system are the gains and losses of passengers, the hiring and loss of staff, and the acquisition of planes. Since buying and selling planes is a simple decision, directly under management control, we do not need to show that on the diagram.
- The problematic flows are the loss of passengers, which appears to be due to a sharp drop in service quality, and the loss of staff, which arose from a steep increase in work pressure.
- The pressure on staff appears to be due to the imbalance between passenger volumes and staff numbers.
- The entire picture explains recent history. Growth in passengers and journeys exceeded the staff's ability to cope, causing them to leave and thus damaging service quality, which in turn increased the loss of passengers.

Valuable insights can arise simply from the team activity involved in developing this picture, as it will typically prompt substantial debate and analysis. Two elements will ensure that insights are accurate and address the correct issues:

- The time charts for core resources, flow drivers, and performance keep discussion focused on the best-known facts of the situation. Do not give up if you do not know precise data; instead, estimate what the facts *might* have been, then use judgment to fill in unknowns. For example, you may not have records of staff attrition rates, but if you know hiring rates and total staff numbers, the history of attrition is easy to calculate.
- You will have quantified how each resource flow depends on the factors driving it. Again, if you do not know for sure what is

happening, think through your best explanation and check that it fits with the facts. Do not tolerate unsubstantiated assertions like "Everyone knows staff are leaving because our competitor offers better pay" unless there is factual evidence to back it up.

Where Is Performance Heading if We Go on Like This?

Exhibit 5.2 goes further than explaining recent history. It sketches out the team's best estimate of where performance is heading into the future. The dashed lines show the estimate that you and your team came up with about the way things are likely to develop if you continue with present policies.

You will continue running a tight operation. This means continuing to hire staff at a steady rate. They may be under pressure, and service quality may not be great, but the business is satisfactory, passengers and journeys are growing, and your company is profitable. You expect that by increasing staff numbers ahead of growth in passengers and journeys, you will gradually bring down the pressure on your staff. In time, service quality will recover enough to slow the loss of passengers and overall growth will pick up.

How Can We Act to Improve Future Performance?

The strategic architecture you develop will enable your team to evaluate a range of possible future strategies—the final stage of the process. You again need an organized approach:

- Start with the points in the business architecture where step 6 showed the challenge to lie: where flows are not running as you would like.
- Focus on the links into that part of the architecture that management can influence. For the airline in Exhibit 5.2, these would be price changes, marketing, and hiring.
- Estimate the scale of policy revision and the likely scale and timing of its results. For example, if you cut fares by 10%, how much would the passenger win rate change? If you double the hiring rate, how quickly will staff numbers rise to your target level?

- Follow the consequences of these policy changes. If you cut fares and bring in more passengers, how much will this change total journeys and pressure on staff? How much impact will *this* have on passenger losses and staff turnover? If you boost hiring, how much will *that* change pressure on staff, and what impact will *that* have on passenger losses and staff turnover?

- Anticipate any issues that might arise from altering the part of the system where the current problem is focused. Cutting your fares will clearly cut revenue per journey, and increasing staff will increase costs, both resulting in a short-term *drop* in profits. How long will it take before the improved resource flows you stimulated work through to generate revenues and profit improvements that overcome this short-term penalty?

- Finally, work through how any performance outcomes might evolve over time because of the proposed changes. The cut in fares might very quickly bring in more passengers and boost revenues and profits, although the *further* consequence would be increased workloads for staff, faster passenger losses, and hence a later decrease in passengers, journeys, revenues, and profits. Alternatively, increasing hiring should reduce the pressure staff are under, reduce turnover, improve service quality, and cut passenger losses, thus increasing total passengers even if there is no change in passenger win rates. More passengers means more journeys and revenues, which will more than pay for the higher staff costs.

Let us work through an example. One of your colleagues believes that poor service quality is unacceptable: It risks building up a poor reputation among potential passengers, which could hurt future growth. This colleague feels you should immediately hire enough staff to remove the overload.

Together, your team works through what might happen (Exhibit 5.3, heavy dotted lines). One risk in the proposed solution is that these newcomers will not know what they are doing at first, so they will be deployed on simple tasks, and hiring rates can be reduced for a while so they can acquire more skill. Your colleague feels that this simple step will immediately relieve some of the pressure and give your people the ability

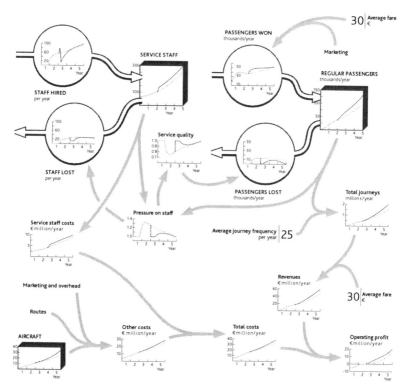

Exhibit 5.3. Relieving Staff Pressure to Improve Service

to improve service quality quickly—especially if you tell them that this is your plan!

You are reasonably confident that the improvements to workload and quality will materialize, so you estimate that passenger growth will accelerate once more, provided you continue adding routes and aircraft. You feel there is a small risk that this will again put staff under pressure some time during year 3. You resolve to keep track of this issue and revisit the hiring policy if it looks as though the problem is recurring.

Take Control: Looking for Fixes

The airline's one-off hiring effort is just one example of a management response to improve performance. There are other common types of response, and it is important to look for and evaluate these in the right order, otherwise you risk undermining one fix by missing unintended consequences:

1. Minimize Leakages in the Resource System

Many organizations focus on cost-effectively acquiring resources and building them but pay much less attention to keeping them. However, there is little advantage in trying to increase the stock of resources in the system if the organization simply loses them again. Too often, customers are won, only to be lost again by poor products or service; staff are hired and trained, only to leave again for any of a host of reasons; new brands are established, only to become uncompetitive as the excitement of the launch fades; distribution agreements are set up, but stall when the company proves unable to sustain the relationship. Of course, there may be situations where the organization has good reason to reduce resources deliberately: for example, cutting back on sales efforts as you progress toward fully exploiting a market opportunity.

2. Improve Resource Acquisition and Development

Once you have ensured there are no leaks in your bath, you can think about filling it!

- Examine each resource inflow, ensuring that other necessary resources, mechanisms, and policies are in place to enable growth. Is the marketing budget sufficient to reach potential customers to make the desired win rate feasible? Is the product's functionality adequate to win customers and are the production, delivery, and installation resources in place to turn orders into completed sales? Is the hiring and training capacity in place to bring in staff at the rate required and make them productive quickly?
- Apply the same principle to ensure that existing resources, mechanisms, and policies are in place to allow resource *development* to occur: turning prototype products into marketable

goods, developing sufficient numbers of experienced people, and so on.

3. Eliminate Self-Imposed Limits

The development of one resource can be hampered by inadequacies in other resources. The team should therefore examine the strategic architecture, focusing on each resource in turn and ascertaining whether its own growth may cause imbalances that restrict its further progress. A valuable question to trigger insight is, "If we are successful in winning these customers (or finding these staff, or launching these products), what are all the things that could go wrong or get in the way?"

4. Look for Reinforcing Mechanisms to Drive Growth

Only after steps 1 through 3 have been completed should you turn to the tempting task of finding reinforcing mechanisms to drive growth. By this point it should be safe to look for ways in which existing resources can be leveraged to drive their own growth or that of others. Can you, for example, leverage existing customers and your resulting reputation to drive faster acquisition of *further* new customers or to increase your ability to hire the best people?

5. Evaluate Step Solutions to Shift the System to a New State

In cases where resource limits and imbalances are serious, it may be impractical or take too long to grow, develop, or reduce the necessary resources. Instead, step changes may be appropriate. These may be limited to actions in a single part of the business or affect many resources simultaneously:

- **Action** may be needed to bring a **single resource into line** with the rest of the system, either as it is or as it is planned to become. Signing up a large new dealership can provide rapid access to a new customer base; licensing products from other firms can quickly fill out a weak product range; and taking on contractors can rapidly relieve staff pressure. Beware, though:

Such actions may themselves place new demands on the organization, so make sure they can be absorbed.

- **Larger actions** may be required to take the business to a whole new level, with better balance and stronger growth potential. Acquisition is one of the clearest examples of such a shift for the whole organization and featured strongly, for example, in the growth of Blockbuster Inc. in its drive to become the dominant movie rental business in the United States and other countries. Each acquisition brought a bucket full of new stores, new customers, and new staff, which were assimilated into the established Blockbuster system. On the other hand, rationalization of several parts of a system may be necessary to bring an ineffective organization back to a core of activity that can be sustained into the future. This may entail rationalizing the product range, removing poor-quality customers, reducing capacity, and cutting staff, all in a coherent move over a short period.

Although step solutions are hardly a new approach to improving an organization's performance, a sound architecture of the situation will provide important safeguards for their implementation. Above all, the rest of the system needs to able to absorb the new or increased resource. It may be necessary to develop complementary resources, or at least start them on an increasing trajectory so that they quickly become able to cope with the influx. Without such precautions, the very solution itself may trigger some new resource losses that undermine your hoped-for improvement.

It is common, for example, for staff to resign after new people arrive. Losses may also arise among other resource categories: For example, inward licensing of new products may cause product development staff to become disillusioned and resign, and the opening of new direct customer relationships may cause dealers to defect to rivals.

Maintain Control: Managing the System

A clear picture of the organization's overall performance and underlying strategic architecture provides valuable insights into how decisions should be guided. The first observation is that using financial outcomes to guide decisions is likely to be hopeless. Clearly, the *immediate* consequences must make sense: You do not want to spend what you cannot afford, or price your product so high as to kill current sales or so low as to destroy margin. But this is not *strategic* control.

A simple principle guides how strategic decisions should be viewed: **Strategic management is all about flow rates!**

To appreciate the implications of this view, think about how our airline team might set a rule of thumb for its marketing spending. Some of the possibilities from which to choose include:

- Marketing spending should not exceed a set fraction of revenue.
- If profits dip too low, cut marketing by a fraction.
- Check that marketing does not exceed a specified cost per passenger journey sold.
- Spend more on marketing if planes are not full.
- Spend more on marketing if regular customers are being lost.

However, marketing *directly* affects just two main items: the frequency with which existing passengers travel with your airline and the rate at which new passengers are won. Marketing is not the *only* factor driving these values, but these values are the only significant things being driven by marketing! These, then, should be the focus of the decision rule for marketing *because they are closely coupled to the decision variable*.

The further you move away from this principle, the more likely it becomes that your decision rule will cause serious problems. It is astonishing, for example, how many organizations stick to "percent of sales" ratios to decide their spending on everything from research and development (R&D) to marketing, training, and maintenance. Just think how this would work for your restaurant:

- Labor cost must not exceed 15% of sales.
- So, if sales fall for some reason, you cut staff.
- So service quality drops, and sales decline.
- So you cut staff again to keep within your 15%!

You become trapped in a cycle of decline. This makes no sense, and in practice, managers usually avoid such foolish consequences. But why *start* with a decision guide that makes no sense in the first place? Pressure from investors who may not understand the structure of the strategic architecture often does not help.

So which performance metrics guide decisions best? Many organizations now use some form of balanced scorecard: an integrated approach to performance measurement and management (Kaplan & Norton, 1996). This recognizes that financial factors alone provide inadequate targets and incentives and so adds measures relating to

- **customers**: satisfaction, retention, market share, and share of business;
- **internal performance**: quality, response times, cost, and new product introductions;
- **learning and growth**: employee satisfaction and availability of information systems.

Only if these additional factors are in good shape will the firm deliver strong financial performance. The balanced scorecard offers important advances over traditional reporting approaches in recognizing the interconnectedness within the business and the importance of measuring and managing "soft" issues. Increasing training of staff about products, for example, will improve sales effectiveness, which in turn will improve sales and margins.

There are limits, though, to the control that a balanced scorecard can achieve if it is not designed to take account of the dynamic interactions that run through the organization's architecture. There are two particularly common failings:

1. What may be good for an indicator under one condition may be bad under other situations. A common example is the winning of new business when the organization cannot cope with what it already has.
2. The optimum balance between different parts of the architecture often shifts substantially as situations develop. Early in the growth of a business, service capacity may need to be a rather minor part of

the organization's total activity, but later it can come to dominate as business builds up. Similarly, you may want to keep staff turnover very low when trying to build capability in a rapidly developing organization, but some rate of staff losses may be positively helpful when growth slows in order to make room for new people to develop.

Doing It Right: Avoiding Disappointment With Strategic Architecture

Management techniques often fail or fall from favor not because they are wrong, but because they are not used properly. Superficial work, done in the hope of a quick fix, is a common culprit. The extensive effort required by many otherwise sound methods is often not sustained. As senior managers instruct their people to undertake one initiative after another, none is carried to fruition before the next is begun. Initiative overload is a common cause of poorly implemented strategies.

Strategy dynamics—the basis of the approach in this book—will not work either if badly applied. It is a powerful but demanding approach that needs to be done professionally and thoroughly if accurate findings and good managerial responses are to be obtained. However, it is not typically more time-consuming or analysis-intensive than many planning processes that organizations put themselves through. Indeed, it often eliminates much activity, data processing, and analysis that would otherwise have been carried out.

Who should do this work? *You and your team.* Continuing management of today's dynamically complex organizations in today's dynamically complex markets and environments is not intuitively easy. For this reason, beware of consultants. Though many excellent professionals can carry out all kinds of demanding analysis and give exceedingly sound advice, few have had a thorough education or training in dynamic analysis. This is a tricky skill, and amateurs will usually get it wrong. Moreover, the need to review your performance dynamics will never go away. You cannot subcontract strategic leadership and you cannot subcontract strategic understanding.

Action Checklist:
Building and Managing the Strategic Architecture

The action checklist for this topic was already outlined, so in summary:

- Follow the steps explained on pages 66–68 to develop the strategic architecture of your organization or for an issue it is facing.
- Using that architecture, follow steps 1 to 5 on pages 75–78 to identify how to enable improved and sustainable performance.

Note that this short book can only provide a summary of how this approach works for some simple business examples. For more extensive guidance on more complex situations, see Warren (2008) and http://www.strategydynamics.com.

CHAPTER 6

You Need Quality Resources as Well as Quantity

Overview

Not all resources of a given type are identical: Customers differ in size and profitability, staff differ in experience, and so on. This chapter will show you the following:

- **how to assess the quality of your resources**
- **how resources bring with them potential access to others**
- **how you can improve resource quality**
- **how to upgrade the quality of an entire strategic architecture**

Assessing the Quality of Resources

Few resources are as uniform as cash: Every dollar bill is the same as all the others. Most resources, however, vary in important ways:

- Customers may be larger or smaller, highly profitable or less so.
- Products may appeal to many customers or few, and satisfy some, many, or all of their needs.
- Staff may have more experience or less, and cost you high salaries or low.

A single resource may even carry several characteristics that influence how the resource stock as a whole affects other parts of the system. Individual bank customers, for example, feature different balances in their accounts, different numbers of products they use from the bank, different levels of risk of defaulting on loans, and so on. **A resource attribute is a characteristic that varies between different items in a single pool of resources.** These differences within each type of resource will themselves change through time. For example, if we lose our most profitable customers our operating profits will fall faster than if we lose only average customers.

If we are to understand *how much* difference such attributes make, it is just as important to measure each resource's attributes as they change through time as it is to measure that resource's overall quantity. Exhibit 6.1 offers some measures that may apply in different cases. The *right* choice of measures will depend on the particular attribute influencing the issue you are concerned with.

We know that managing resources is tricky because they fill and drain away over time and depend on each other. To this challenge we must now add the problem that when a resource is won or lost, it brings or takes these attributes with it.

Tangible resource	Attributes	Possible attribute measures
Customers	Purchase rate	$/year
Staff	Experience Skill level	Years Fraction of tasks that can be done
Distributors	Market reach	End customers served
Transport fleet vehicles	Capacity	Maximum passengers or load
Production facilities	Capacity	Units/year
A bank's loans	Value Interest margin Risk	€thousand Percent Probability of default
A supermarket chain's branches	Catchment population	Thousand people
A pharmaceuticals firm's drugs portfolio	Potential patients to benefit	People

Exhibit 6.1. Examples of Attributes for Certain Resources

Moreover, attributes may be potential rather than actual and still require efforts on our part if they are to be developed. Opening a new retail store, for example, brings with it access to the population around that store. Those potential customers will only become *actual* customers if our stores provide attractive products, prices, and service.

Understanding Resource Attributes

Consider a firm concerned that it has too many small customers. To picture the extent of the problem, take the annual revenue contributed by the largest customer alone and add to it the contribution from the second largest, then the third, and so on. If we carry on doing this until the entire customer base is accounted for, we get a curve of cumulative revenue versus cumulative customers (Exhibit 6.2).

Not only is this a record of the present situation, but it can also be used to decide policy. The extent of the "tail" of small customers is visible, and average customer revenue can be easily calculated. Managers can discuss the relative merits of pruning the customer base by various degrees:

- If the customer base is reduced, what reduction in support costs should be feasible?
- What is the risk that cutting off small customers may cause others to leave?

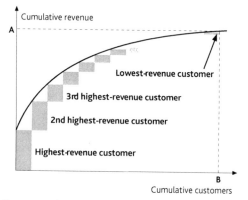

Exhibit 6.2. Revenue-Generating Profile of a Customer Base

- Could we inadvertently strengthen rivals by giving them a more viable business with the customers we are abandoning?
- What is the scope for replacing poor customers with better ones?

It is important, however, to focus on the *correct* attribute for the intended purpose. Customer revenue is one useful measure but does not necessarily correspond to customer *profitability*. Exhibit 6.3 shows the link between the two attributes. It includes loss-makers: The positive contribution from the profitable customers on the left is partly negated by the losses from unprofitable customers on the right.

Here are two common observations to bear in mind:

1. The biggest customer (or product, or salesperson) is often not the biggest contributor to profit. The biggest customers, for example,

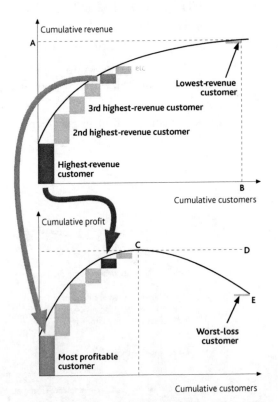

Exhibit 6.3. Profitability Profile of a Customer Base

often drive the hardest bargain on price, and may even be *unprof-itable* to serve. The products that best meet customers' needs may incur higher than average production costs or require heavy service support. And one law firm found that its star partner who brought in the most clients actually produced *losses* for the firm by underpricing the work sold to them!

2. Conversely, the customers (products or staff) who contribute most to profitability may not be the biggest.

You may need to think more widely about which attributes are important, apart from revenue and profit contribution. Most banks, for example, are engaged in a competitive pursuit of individuals with high net worth. These customers have large potential deposits and borrowing needs on which a bank can make a good margin. However, they are also the best informed and least loyal of customers, often following the best deals from bank to bank. Far from being the most valuable customers, they can be the most costly to serve.

The shape of the curves in Exhibit 6.3 should not simply be accepted as given but should be challenged. The airline industry offers a dramatic example. Customers who were willing to pay only low fares have been unprofitable to the major carriers for decades; they were far to the right on Exhibit 6.3. Southwest, Ryanair, easyJet, and the others rewrote the rule book, and the profit curve kept on climbing as more customers were added. They lifted point E above point D.

There can be a limit to this potential, however, especially if fierce competition develops. In an effort to push revenues and profits still higher, these airlines risk extending the curves far out to the right. Sure, you might be able to capture another 1,000 customers by offering flights for $10, but if those passengers now cost more to win and serve than they contribute, they generate very little revenue and negative profits. This certainly proved to be the case for those banks who got overenthusiastic in offering subprime mortgages in the years up to 2008.

The tail of problem customers can completely wipe out the contribution from the profitable ones: Point E in Exhibit 6.3 can drop below zero. Such situations are especially punishing, and not simply because the business is unprofitable overall. The problematic resources impose heavy demands on the rest of the system and take up managers' attention.

In retailing, for example, unprofitable branches are often disproportionately costly in terms of delivery, are frequently left with the least able management, and suffer from high staff turnover. Both McDonald's (in the years up to 2002) and Starbucks (prior to 2005) fell into this trap, and both had to dig their way out of the problem caused by overexpansion. As the returning CEO of McDonald's said in 2002, "We are in transition from a company that emphasizes 'adding restaurants to customers' to one that emphasizes 'adding customers to restaurants'" (McDonald's Corporation, 2003). This will continue to be a challenging issue for Blockbuster to manage as its stores suffer erosion of their sales by postal and online movie supply services.

Managing the Profit Distribution Curve

Exhibit 6.3 is an improvement on Exhibit 6.2 but must still be handled with care. It may be unwise to eliminate all customers to the right of point C, for several reasons:

- **It may not be possible to cut overheads in line with customer numbers**. Eliminating all customers between points C and E would simply raise the overhead burden on the profitable customers to the left. The curve could be squashed to the left but with the profit peak at an even lower level than point E.
- **Individual resources often develop along the quality curve**. Banks know that they have to put up with unreliable and unprofitable students because when they get good jobs, they will become less risky and their financial needs will develop.
- **Poor resources may be linked to good ones**. Banks take good care of nuisance youngsters for another reason: Their parents are often customers. If banks are too hard on the kids, they risk losing profitable business from the parents.

These cautionary points should not be overstated. When people argue that customers or products are interdependent and have great potential, take care to make an objective assessment. Do they *really* have great potential? Would you *really* lose some important business if you removed them?

Finally, note that it may be possible to do good business serving customers that, for other companies, are unattractive. The large information technology (IT) service providers such as EDS, Infosys, and CSC, for example, would not be interested for a moment in serving small business clients, but there is a thriving market for small computer support service providers among those same small clients. Taken to the extreme, it is even possible to develop attractive business models that focus exclusively on serving the poorest customers (Prahalad, 2006).

Managing Resource Attributes: The "Coflow" Structure

If we are to add a clear picture of resource attributes to our strategic architecture, we need to capture their dynamics accurately. Three mechanisms cause attribute levels to change:

1. **Directly increasing the attribute** without making any change to the tangible resource itself. Banks, for example, may win a larger share from existing customers by getting more of their savings or borrowing requirements.

2. **Obtaining new, better quality resources with more of the desired attribute**. This raises the *average* quality of our total resource pool. Bringing in poorer quality resources, on the other hand, dilutes the average quality. As noted above, many retailers have fallen into the trap of adding stores that reach fewer and fewer new customers. Similarly, low-fare airlines are struggling to find as yet undeveloped routes that attract sufficient new passengers to be worthwhile.

3. **Losing resources that have too little of the desired attribute**. This raises the average quality of those that remain; for example, dropping unprofitable customers or discontinuing unpopular products.

These three mechanisms are all positive, raising the quality of the resource in question, but each has a negative counterpart. An attribute may simply decline, as when staff forget key skills, be diluted by adding lower quality items (hiring unskilled staff), or disappear, as when a high-quality resource is lost (losing skilled staff).

This process is captured by a framework known as a "coflow," so called because the inflow of a given resource (staff, say) brings with it a *connected flow* of its attribute (their skill). Similar effects occur for many other resources in many other contexts (Sterman, 2000, chap. 12).

Let us go back to the example of your restaurant from earlier chapters. Imagine that it starts to win more customers, but these new customers eat with you less often than your regulars do (Exhibit 6.4). Regular customers all visited eight times per month, but these new people only visit five times per month. After one month of adding 50 customers per month, you now have 550 regulars. If they visited as often as the 500 initial customers, you

Doing It Right: How to Think About Attributes

A helpful way to think about an attribute builds on the idea of resources as water in a bathtub. You can think of the attribute as the *heat* the water holds:

- If your bath is too cold, you can raise the temperature by turning on the hot tap. The hotter the new water is, the less you have to add to raise the overall temperature.
- You could also add heat by putting a heater in the bath (do not try this for real!). Product obsolescence, a decline in your customers' business, and staff forgetting their skills can be thought of as your bath cooling down. Management, however, works like a heater directly in the bath: training can be used to raise skill levels, product development to improve the product range, and business development to boost the profitability of an account base.
- Lastly, resources have a neat characteristic that bath water does not share: You can selectively remove the coldest water (the least skilled staff, the worst customer accounts, the least successful products) and so leave hotter water behind. You cannot do this with your bath, but you can with your organization's resources.

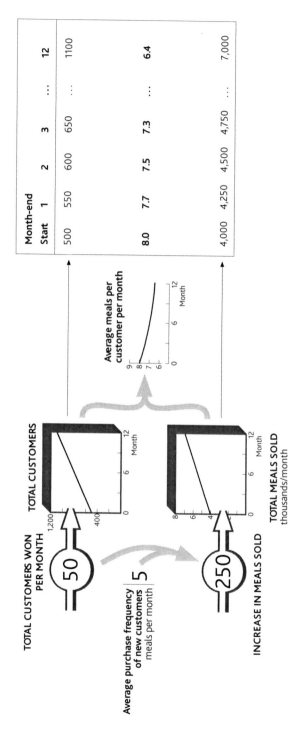

Month-end	Start	1	2	3	...	12
	500	550	600	650	...	1100
	8.0	7.7	7.5	7.3	...	6.4
	4,000	4,250	4,500	4,750	...	7,000

Average meals per customer per month

TOTAL CUSTOMERS WON PER MONTH

50

TOTAL CUSTOMERS

Average purchase frequency of new customers
meals per month

5

250

INCREASE IN MEALS SOLD

TOTAL MEALS SOLD
thousands/month

Exhibit 6.4. Dilution of Average Client Quality

would be selling at the rate of 4,400 meals per month. Instead, these 50 new people bring just 250 extra meals per month, so on average your customers are now visiting just over 7.7 times per month.

This framework does have an important limitation, in that you lose some of the detail by lumping all these customers together. Inside the stock of 550 customers at the end of month 1, for example, there may be some making 12 visits per month, others 10 per month, others 8 per month, and so on. To see this detail you would need to build a quality

Doing It Right: Calculating Average Attributes

You might think that the easiest way to work out these attributes is to put their *average* quantity in the stock that "coflows" with the resource. In Exhibit 6.4, surely you should show the *average* meals per customer in the resource tank instead of the *total* meals sold per month. Unfortunately it is very difficult to work out the numbers that way.

The lower tank in such cases (total meals sold per month) is keeping a check on the total *heat* in your bathtub. This can have some curious effects. For example, if you want to track employees' average experience, your resource stock carries the number of staff, say 200, and the lower stock carries their *total combined experience*: say 2,200 person-years. The average experience is thus the resource quantity divided by the attribute quantity, that is, 2,200/200 = 11 years.

A further result of this approach is that it can lead you seemingly to break the rules of what is or is not a resource. Telecom firms, for example, track average revenue per user (ARPU). If you have 1.5 million subscribers, each giving you an average of $40 per month in revenue, then the 1.5 million subscribers go in the top tank, but the bottom tank holds $60 million per month, that is, your *total* revenue. ARPU is thus the ratio between these two stocks. "But surely," you may remind us, "we agreed in chapter 2 that revenue is not a resource?" It is not; we are using it here only to track an important quality of the subscribers.

If the telecom firm wants a higher ARPU, it has three options: increase the average revenue from existing customers, add higher usage customers, or lose low-revenue customers.

curve like that in Exhibit 6.2. But this can mean extra work, so **explore the detailed resource quality profile (Exhibit 6.2) only if it is essential to answer the specific issue of concern.**

Problems Caused by Resource Attributes

Understanding resource attributes and how to manage them gives you still more control over the performance you can develop from your business architecture. But you also need to be conscious of the troubles they can cause. Some of the most common challenges that attributes produce are as follows:

- **Resources only bring *access* to other resources**, which means that you still have to work to develop them. In Exhibit 6.4, your restaurant attracted new customers and you immediately enjoyed new sales. But such immediacy does not always apply. Sometimes resources bring with them only *potential* resources that we then have to develop if we are to turn them into *active* resources. A new product may bring with it the possibility of serving the needs of many new customers, but we still have to *develop* these customers. A newly appointed dealer may provide access to new end users for our products, but that dealer still has to sell the benefits to them before they will become active users.
- **Potential resources can dry up**. I mentioned in chapter 3 that managers can easily be blind to the drying up of potential resources; now we have the further problem that any resources that *do* remain are likely to be of poorer quality too. This challenge of diminishing returns is often simply ignored. It is more comfortable to assume that the great opportunity associated with the early expansion of our business is going to continue on the same attractive trajectory.
- **Cannibalization can set in**. To these two problems we must add a third: cannibalization. There will come a point when new routes opened by an airline start to divert active passengers away from existing routes. Leisure travelers in particular select from

a range of possible destinations, so if you add a new one, some people will probably migrate to the new offering. The bigger you get, the more this is going to happen. So resource items that were originally high in quality deteriorate as you take more away from them.

Action Checklist: Upgrading Your Resources

As you assess how your organization is doing and where it may be capable of going, extend your thinking beyond the *quantity* of resources that you have and can win and focus on their *quality*. Obvious resources to view in this way include customers, staff, and products.

- Consider the **attributes** of the resources you currently have. What exactly is the quality of each resource, and how is this quality distributed? Do you have a uniformly valuable group of key staff, products, or customers, for example, or do you rely on a handful of stars?
- Find out how those qualities are **changing**. Are your customer base and revenue growing but only through the addition of low-value business? Or are you making inroads into really good-quality customers? At what rate do you hope to improve that quality over time and to what level?
- How **healthy** are your resources overall? Do you have low-value customers, marginally valued products, and staff working unproductively to support these poor-quality resources? If so, you may have to consider rationalizing the whole system to a smaller but more powerful and competitive core.
- Consider **potential** resources. Are you focusing on building business with a new potential resource, but failing to capture that potential? Or is there an opportunity to use new markets or products, that bring with them the chance to reach out to new customers?
- Finally, be sure you are not approaching any quality **problems**. Is any potential resource in danger of running out? Are resources declining in quality? Is there a danger of resources

cannibalizing each other? If any of these problems are approaching, can you do anything to escape their grip, or do you have to recognize the resulting limits and begin reconfiguring your organization?

Remember, the only way to understand what these phenomena really mean for your organization is to work out the numbers.

CHAPTER 7

Managing Rivalry for Customers and Other Resources

Overview

Building your own resources is challenging enough, but competitors are not going to sit by and let you take what you want without a fight. Even in nonbusiness situations, we struggle to win people, supporters, cash, and other resources. This chapter considers how to win, develop, and retain resources, and shows how rivalry plays out through time. This chapter will do the following:

- **explain the three dominant forms of rivalry**: turning potential customers into actual customers, capturing rivals' customers, and competing for sales to shared customers
- **show how these processes work**, both on their own and in combination, and describe the challenge facing managers in deciding where to act to win these battles

Types of Rivalry

We mostly think about rivalry in the context of competitive markets for goods and services. Discussions of competitiveness often focus on high-level measures such as sales growth and market share. However, these are not factors over which we can have any direct effect, but are the *results* of success in winning, developing, and retaining important resources.

Since most of what we know about rivalry comes from studies of price- and value-based markets, it is perhaps not surprising that customer markets grab all the attention. This focus has a most unfortunate consequence: competitive strategy seems to have little relevance for nonprofit sectors such as public services, the voluntary sector, and nongovernmental organizations (NGOs). Yet nothing could be further from the truth; these organizations constantly compete for resources. Skilled staff are the obvious example, but supporters, cash, and other resources must also be battled for.

Nevertheless, customers are still the most obvious resource that must be won and retained against rivals, so this is where we will focus first. However, most of the principles explained here are readily applicable to rivalry for staff and some other resources as well.

There are three main forms of rivalry, which sometimes operate alone but more often play out alongside each other:

- Type 1: The battle to win *new* customers who do not yet buy your kind of product from anyone (potential customers).
- Type 2: The struggle to capture *existing* customers from rivals while keeping your own customers from switching to rivals.
- Type 3: The fight for the best possible *share* of business from customers who are not exclusively with you or anyone else.

Let us see how these three mechanisms operate with a popular example.

Barbie Fights for Her Crown

For more than 40 years, Barbie dominated the kingdom of dolls. More than a billion Barbie dolls (including her relatives) have been sold since 1959. Mattel sells 1.5 million dolls every week in more than 140 countries. But Barbie's undisputed reign was attacked by a new family of would-be royalty: the Disney Princesses. Snow White, Sleeping Beauty, Tinkerbell, and their friends put aside their differences in a concerted attempt to win the hearts of children ages 3 to 7. During their most spectacular period of success, sales of Princesses grew from $136 million in 2001 to $700 million in 2002. Sales of Princess dolls alone were running at 4 million per year—already a substantial incursion into Barbie's 75 million.

So how did Barbie resist this attack on her supremacy? She had three battles to fight at once. First, she needed to keep winning the hearts of the youngest children buying a fashion doll for the first time (or persuading their parents to do so). Second, she needed to keep the loyalty of existing Barbie owners and hope they did not relegate her to the cupboard to make room for the Princesses. Third, she would have preferred not even to share space on the bedroom carpet with them.

Barbie had limited resources: only so many sales and marketing people to defend her kingdom, only so much shelf space in stores where she could reach the children she wished to make her loyal owners, and only so much cash to spend on advertising, promotion, and pricing. If she did nothing, her position would continue to be eroded as the battle went against her on all three fronts.

Type 1 Rivalry: Competing for Potential Customers

As new potential customers develop, rivals fight to win them for their own business. They also seek to develop this potential pool of resources. Let us take a starting position in which Barbie has some 100 million active owners. Before the invasion of the Princesses, the situation was relatively stable; say she was winning about 20 million new owners a year but losing a similar number of older girls. Doll sales come both from first-time buyers and from repeat purchases by girls who already own Barbie. There is much additional revenue from sales of accessories, so if she loses this fight for doll sales, that income will also be lost.

One scenario for this part of the Princesses' incursion is that they quickly increase the fraction of small girls who choose *them* rather than Barbie as their preferred first-time fashion doll. Princess sales, too, will reflect both the rate at which first-time owners are buying these dolls and the repeat purchase rate from girls who already own one or more of the collection. If this scenario happens, the Princesses will succeed in taking a large part of Barbie's domain without having to fight for her *existing* loyal owners at all (Exhibit 7.1).

Later, though, the novelty of being the first to own a Princess has faded so that new owners in 2 or 3 years' time once again increasingly choose Barbie (Exhibit 7.2).

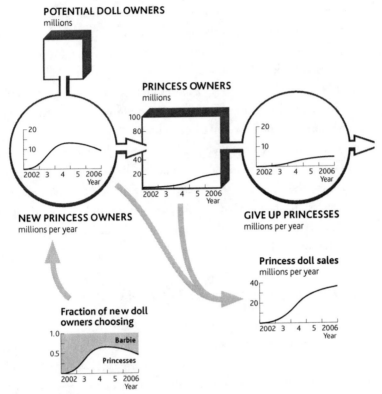

Exhibit 7.1. Princesses Capture an Increasing Fraction of New Doll Owners

The following are two points to note:

1. Children are slow to give up Princesses in these early years because relatively few have grown tired of them.
2. Sales of dolls reflect both first-time purchases and additional dolls bought by children who already own one. With so many members of this extended royal family, these numbers could be large.

The number of Barbie's loyal owners would therefore be reduced by the same numbers as are won by the Princesses.

The challenge for organizations that are developing potential customers is to understand what is driving customers' choice of which "pipe" to flow through. Their choices will be driven by competitors' decisions and actions, especially

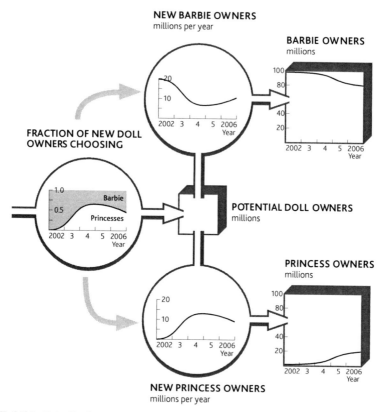

Exhibit 7.2. Barbie's Loss of New Owners to the Princesses

- marketing and sales activities;
- relative price;
- relative perceived performance of competing products.

To these can be added further mechanisms, such as word of mouth driving reinforcing growth—here, Princess owners encouraging their friends to buy Princesses too—and availability of Princesses in stores.

Type 2 Rivalry: Competing for Rivals' Customers

Competitors battle to steal resources that have already been developed and are controlled by their rivals at the same time as they fight to prevent their own resources from being lured away. The rate at which customers choose to leave one firm for another reflects the comparison of price and benefits (value for money) between the rivals. This flow of customers between competing suppliers may, however, be moderated by switching costs.

Barbie's predicament would be still worse if, as well as losing out in the battle for new doll owners, she found that her *existing* owners started deserting her too. Again, we do not know how this trend might develop, but one scenario is that the fraction leaving her rises steadily through time (Exhibit 7.3).

Notice that the *number* of children switching per year stops growing in spite of the rising *fraction* who do so, simply because there are fewer left to be lost! Indeed, if we continued this scenario, the switching rate would drop to zero as the pool of former Barbie owners empties. We could speculate on all kinds of other scenarios. Barbie could, for example,

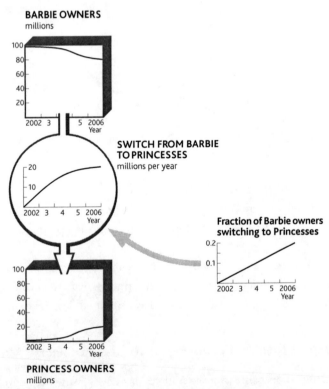

Exhibit 7.3. A Rising Fraction of Barbie Owners Switches to Princesses

see a rapid early loss as the least loyal Barbie owners switch, followed by a slowdown as only her most loyal subjects remain. The exact story behind the battle makes a big difference to how both Barbie and the Princesses should react.

Type 2 rivalry has certain features that can be understood only by tracking and understanding what is driving these switch rates. First, switching accelerates as the customer benefits move further ahead of the cost of switching. Like the take-up costs for first-time doll owners, the switching costs involved if Barbie's existing owners abandon her and take up with the Princesses instead, are probably small. However, the quantity of Barbie dolls and accessories already in the toy cupboard may impose storage challenges, as well as inducing parental resistance to switching! In other cases, switching costs can be considerable. Owners of game consoles accumulate expensive libraries of game titles, plus networks of friends with whom they share enthusiasm for their particular platform. Persuading *these* consumers to switch is much tougher.

Many markets feature a group of hard-to-persuade customers who fail to move despite strong inducements, either because of emotional reasons, such as loyalty or comfort, or because of simple inertia. The deregulation of utility markets was supposed to encourage the mass migration of customers from inefficient incumbent suppliers to the many new entrants who would offer competitive prices. In practice, many customers failed to switch in spite of the prospect of considerable savings.

Type 2 rivalry increases in importance as markets develop. Firms are fighting to pull customers out of their rivals' resource systems and into their own, so the more customers are in *that* state (rather than in an undeveloped potential pool), the more intense Type 2 rivalry becomes. Customers benefit from a range of incentives to stay or join, which is why regulatory competition policies focus so strongly on eliminating switching costs.

As with the race to develop potential customers, it is often necessary to understand customer switching between multiple competitors. This can be achieved by grouping competitors and tracking the few most likely to attack your firm or most vulnerable to attack from you.

Doing It Right: Dynamic Market Intelligence

It is surprisingly rare for firms to have good competitive intelligence on customer migration behavior, even when the information is readily to hand. Moreover, few firms make explicit choices about which rivals to defend against and which to attack. Instead, the external competitive environment is generally treated as a uniform whole, to and from which customers are won and lost in an indiscriminate manner.

This will not do! The following are questions to ask:

- To which specific rivals are you losing which particular customers, at what rate, and why? What do you need to change, by how much, to reduce that loss rate, to what extent?
- From which specific rivals can you capture the greatest rate of which particular customers and why? What do you need to change, by how much, to increase that win rate, to what extent?

Type 3 Rivalry: Competing for Sales to Shared Customers

In Type 1 and Type 2 rivalry, we have assumed that all customers purchase exclusively from one firm or another. This is true only in certain markets. Mobile phone subscribers hardly ever use two services, for example, and most households purchase electricity from a single supplier.

In many markets, however, customers tend to allocate buying between two or more suppliers. In these cases, rivals are fighting for a larger *share* of sales to customers who purchase from several suppliers. Since these customers already buy from more than one source, the cost of switching for any single buying decision is generally low. Share of sales can therefore swing quickly between rivals. One market where competition for sales to shared customers takes place is fast-moving consumer goods such as food and drink. Let us see how Type 3 rivalry could affect the battle between Barbie and the Princesses.

We start with the rather obvious point that customers probably only *become* owners of both rivals' products if they first own one or the other. It is unlikely (but not impossible) that a small child will buy, or be given, her first Barbie *and* her first Princess on the same occasion. This means that the stock of shared owners fills up from Barbie owners getting their first Princess, plus Princess owners getting their first Barbie (Exhibit 7.4). One reason for this latter process to be more evident than the former is that Barbie appeals to a rather older age group than Princesses.

This new pool of shared owners could be helpful or harmful to Barbie in her fight for sales. The Princess owners who buy Barbie for the first time may prefer playing with Barbie and her friends and may even end up putting their Princesses away completely. Equally, the opposite could happen. Barbie's loyal owners who buy their first Princess get to enjoy this new toy and start buying more of them, perhaps giving up Barbie entirely.

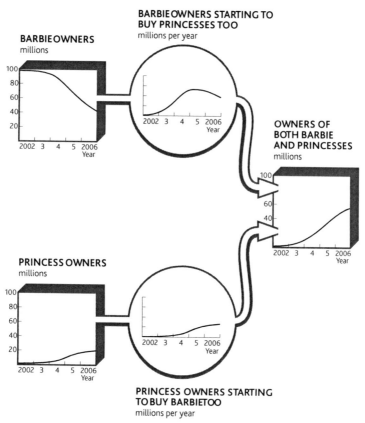

Note: For clarity, other flows of doll owners are not shown.
Exhibit 7.4. Owners of Barbie or Princesses Become Owners of Both

This new mechanism changes our view of the Type 2 rivalry described in Exhibit 7.3. That picture implied that children will abandon Barbie on the same day they take up with the Princesses and vice versa. Possible though that is, it is more likely that the switch from dedicated Barbie owner to dedicated Princess owner will happen gradually, through a period of being an active owner of both.

This new pool of shared owners complicates matters when we try to understand Barbie's sales rate. She now enjoys sales from four distinct sources (Exhibit 7.5):

1. Those first-time buyers of any fashion doll who choose Barbie
2. Repeat purchases from dedicated Barbie owners
3. First-time Barbie purchases from children who previously owned only Princesses
4. Repeat purchases from children who own both Barbie and Princesses

Child's Play: Managing Competitive Dynamics

The explanation for Barbie's sales through time hardly seems obvious or easy. The problem of working out exactly what to do about all these customer flows and sales rates is still more complex. The numbers involved in Barbie's case will be huge. Advertising budgets of millions of dollars will be allocated by both firms, supporting the efforts of many talented and costly people. A daunting list of vital questions faces these executives. For example,

- How much should we spend on advertising in each geographic market?
- How much should we spend on in-store promotion?
- How much sales effort should we devote to winning new stores to stock our products?
- How should we set the normal price for our dolls and their accessories?
- How much should we spend on special offers?
- On which advertising channels should we spend how much money in order to reach which group of potential or already active owners?

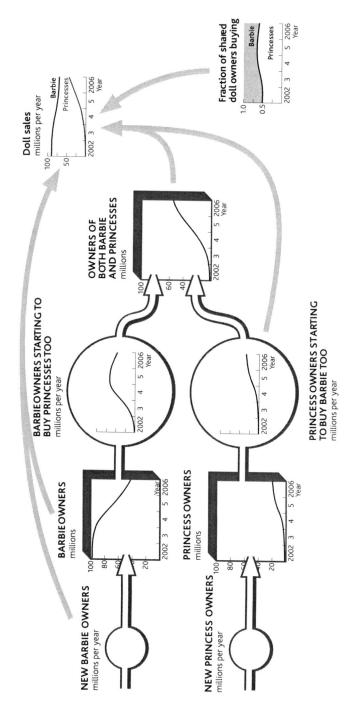

Exhibit 7.5. Sources of Barbie Sales When Children May Own Both Types of Dolls

And remember that all these decisions, and more, have to recognize that we want to be *profitable* too, so spending more on everything is not an option.

You *could* draw up some broad guidelines and hope they will work. But the chance that these guesses will be anywhere near what would be best is small. You will probably spend large sums of money and effort trying to make something change that will not, put too little effort into moving something that can and should be moved, or do both repeatedly.

If you *really* want to work out what is best to do at any moment *and* understand how these best decisions develop through time, then you have no alternative but to find the information on customer flows and choices. Then you must identify how your actions and efforts (along with those of your rivals) are constantly altering these behaviors. Only by using continuous market intelligence on these resources and flows will you be able to make sound decisions on the complex questions of customer rivalry.

The decisive case for taking on these questions and doing the work to find out what is happening and why arises from a point we stressed before—**strategic management is all about the flow rates!** This is why major global companies are switching their strategic marketing planning to a strategy dynamics basis.

Action Checklist: Understanding and Managing Competition Over Time

Here are some tips for understanding what is happening in the battle between you and your competitors:

- Start with a chart of what has happened, and is likely to happen, to your own customer base, not just how many there are in each period, but also how many are won and lost.
- For customers you win, identify the rate at which some of these are won from a potential population of previously inactive customers and how many are won from rivals. If

you have more than one competitor, focus attention first on those that offer the biggest threat—or biggest opportunity.

- Try to estimate or research the same information for your rivals.
- Do not forget to include the pool of shared customers who are not loyal to either you or a competitor. Together with the previous steps, this will give you a complete view of which customers and potential customers are moving at what rate among the alternatives.
- Identify what effect your decisions, and your competitors', have to drive customers to move, at the rates they do, between the alternative available states.

If you sell through intermediaries, such as a consumer goods company selling through retailers, you will need to do the same work for those intermediaries as well as for final customers.

This may all seem a big effort, and a big change from how you currently do things, but remember, this *is* how the world works, so if you try making decisions without this insight, you will struggle to make the right choices. And remember, your competitors may be ahead of you in this thinking.

CHAPTER 8

Intangible Resources and Capabilities

Overview

Earlier chapters explained how a few simple resources lie at the heart of any organization, determining how it performs through time. These systems contain *people*, though, and people have feelings and capabilities that determine how they behave: doing more or less of what you would like, or deciding to change from one state to another. This chapter explains the following:

- **why intangible factors matter**, and what you can do to understand, measure, and manage them
- **how intangibles behave through time**, responding to influences from elsewhere
- **the impact of capabilities in driving business performance**
- **how intangibles influence the core architecture** of simpler tangible factors

Why Intangibles Matter

Soft factors play a crucial role in competitive performance—motivated staff are more productive than those with poor morale, a strong reputation in the market helps customer acquisition, a charity that enjoys its donors' commitment will raise money more easily, and a political party with stronger support among the electorate will get more votes. If we are to improve performance over time, then we have no choice but to understand how to assess and influence these soft factors (Carmelli, 2004; Hall, 1992). The logic is unavoidable:

- Performance at each moment depends on the tangible resources you can access.
- The only way to change performance is to build and sustain these resources.
- So, if soft factors are to make any difference to performance (which they clearly do), they *must* do so by affecting your firm's ability to capture and hold on to these same tangible resources.

Unfortunately, intangibles can be tough to manage. You may easily borrow cash, buy production capacity, or hire staff, but it is slow and difficult to build staff morale, a strong reputation, or support from your donors or voters.

Once you have a strong intangible, it will speed the growth of other resources, so imagine the likely performance advantage for an organization with an edge in *all* such factors. Even better, since it is often hard for competitors to see from outside exactly what these intangibles are and to work out how to collect them, they can give you a *sustainable* advantage.

Measuring Intangible Resources

A senior partner at a major global management consultancy once told me, "We don't include intangible items in our client work, because they are undetectable, unmeasurable, and unmanageable." Wrong on all three counts!

The atmosphere in a company where people are confident and motivated feels quite different from that in an organization where staff are under pressure. In the same way, salespeople know the difference in a customer's reaction when they try to sell products with a bad reputation, and CEOs certainly notice the hostility of investors who have lost confidence in their management.

Organizations increasingly measure intangible factors. Product and service quality, staff skills, and motivation now commonly feature in management reports. Even investor sentiment is regularly tracked and scrutinized by many companies.

The achievements of exemplary managers in difficult situations make it clear that the third accusation—that intangibles are unmanageable—is also untrue. Effective factory managers can improve product quality; inspirational sales managers can boost sales force morale and confidence; capable chief executives can reassure anxious investors.

All that is lacking in most cases is a clear link between changes to these critical items and the organization's performance. Executives know these things matter but need a clearer picture of *how* they work and *how much*.

How to Measure Intangible Factors

Some intangibles have simple measures, as shown in Exhibit 8.1. If you have such measures, use them instead of talking in generalities. Performance outcomes cannot be understood through qualitative comments like "We have highly motivated staff" or "Our delivery performance is excellent." Worse still, we often find management making such comments with no factual evidence to back them up or even when there is evidence to the contrary!

Many soft factors can be measured on a 0 to 1 scale, where 0 means a complete absence of the resource and 1 is the maximum level you can imagine. Here are some tips:

- **Pick the measure that matters**. Many soft issues lend themselves to a range of different measures. Product quality, for example, could be how well the product performs its purpose for the customer, how long it lasts before failing, the fraction of units produced that have to be rejected, and so on. So which of these measures (or others) should you be using? The key is to pick the measure (or measures) that most directly affects the next factor you are trying to explain. So, for example, how well the product performs its purpose will affect customer win rates;

Intangible resource	Common measure	Units
Product quality	Failure rate	Fraction per month
Delivery reliability	Order completeness	Fractions of orders fulfilled
Investor support	Research results	0 to 1.0
Staff morale	Research results	0 to 1.0

Exhibit 8.1. Measures for Some Intangible Resources

the failure rate in use will probably affect customer loss rates; and the reject fraction will affect the average production cost of accepted units.

- **People do not tell it like it is**. You cannot rely on getting accurate answers from people you question. There are many reasons for this. They may give you the answers that they think you want to hear: "How was your meal?" "Fine, thanks." They may not want to appear ignorant or foolish; they may say they bought their last car because it offered great value when the issue that really swung it was the color or the cup holders. Research professionals understand that surveys are not entirely reliable, and they use a range of methods to get closer to real motivations. There is a limit, though, to how confident you can be in such results, so you may have to cross-check your findings against other information and keep checking!

- **Do not use consequences as measures**. This is one of the most common mistakes. We do not have good information on how staff feel they are valued, say, so we use the staff turnover rate as a measure of motivation. However, staff turnover could be driven by a host of factors apart from people's feelings of being valued. You should track the factor itself, not just its consequences.

- **Monitor how the reference level for intangible factors changes over time**. A great product is quickly matched by competitors, so customers come to expect this standard. Flexible employment terms make working for you seem highly appealing to new employees but are soon taken for granted. So watch out for the reference against which people are comparing: This may be what they have previously experienced, what competitors offer, or what they think *should* be possible.

Dealing With Intangibles

A clue that you are dealing with an intangible resource comes when the word "perceived" features in your likely explanation for what is going on. Perceived menu quality is key, for example, to a restaurant's ability to win new customers, because those people do not have any direct experience of

Doing It Right: When Is Quality a Resource?

It is easy to view quality as a driver of customers' decisions, but certain qualities do not exhibit the characteristics of a resource, meaning they do not fill up gradually over time. For example, if you run a call center that has enough trained staff to handle 1,000 calls per hour, quality will be fine so long as calls arrive at this rate or less. However, if 1,100 calls per hour start arriving, quality will drop instantly. If call rates drop again, quality will quickly recover.

Failure rates or faults in manufactured items, on the other hand, have to be worked at over time, with managers constantly seeking to identify and remove the sources of the problem. This quality, then, *does* fill up gradually, reaching a limit as it approaches 1. Continual improvement has been the motivation for many quality initiatives such as total quality management and six sigma.

From this it may seem that service qualities respond immediately, and product qualities behave like resources. Unfortunately, things are not quite that simple. If you have plenty of staff, but your service quality reflects levels of skill, then this quality too will gradually improve or deteriorate over time. In this case, the correct approach would be to capture the resource of staff skill, which is filled up by training and drains away when staff leave or forget.

what they will be served until they have actually eaten there. The perceived appeal of working in the media industry is key to encouraging young people to seek a job with radio and TV companies. The perceived quality of management is vital for entrepreneurs to win over investors. This is hardly a new idea; the core principle in cognitive psychology is that **state of mind drives behavior**.

There are two kinds of behavior that particularly interest us in so far as they affect the overall performance of our organizations:

1. **People choosing to switch from one state to another**: for example, deciding to stop being your customer, to become an investor, or to join your staff

2. **People choosing to do more or less of something**: for example, using eBay to buy and sell items on line more frequently, sending more text messages by mobile phone, or working harder

Sometimes these choices are helpful—when people choose to join you or do more of what you want—and sometimes they are unhelpful. Negative situations occur where people do more of what you *do not* want: such as customers denigrating your company to others, or staff criticizing your efforts to make important changes.

Problems Caused by Soft Factors

The Case of the IT Service Firm

To understand how feelings drive people to change from one state to another, consider the example of a medium-size information technology (IT) service firm that found itself in trouble. It was losing its best clients, who complained of poor service and was also having trouble winning new business. To make matters worse, vital, skilled staff were leaving. Yet just a couple of years earlier, the firm had exhibited none of these problems and had been enjoying modest growth.

The trouble seemed to lead back to the arrival of a new head of sales and marketing, who had surveyed the firm's market and found plenty of potential clients who wanted the kind of service support the firm offered. Until then, growth had largely come from occasional referrals by satisfied clients. The new guy convinced his colleagues they were missing a great opportunity and set about launching a sales campaign. Sure enough, he brought in new clients at a good rate (Exhibit 8.2).

This new person had recently left, frustrated by the difficulty he was now having in winning new business and irritated by the growing distrust of the rest of the team. They were worried about what was happening and how to fix it. In particular, client losses had jumped to unacceptable rates and service quality had suffered—calls for help went unanswered and fixes that were done failed to solve customers' problems. Moreover, the decrease in client acquisition did not seem to have been caused by market conditions; there was still plenty of potential business to be had.

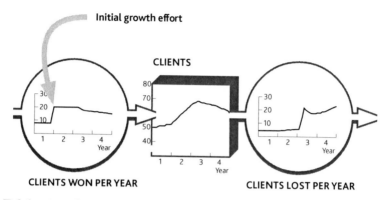

Exhibit 8.2. A Service Firm's Problem With Winning and Keeping Clients

Calls to potential clients revealed that the firm had not won this business because of rumors about its poor quality.

Examining the quality problem first, the team confirmed what they already suspected, that the service staff had been under mounting pressure from the extra work required to serve all the new clients. They could cope with this pressure at first because they were not especially stretched, but a year or so later it got to be too much for them and they started making mistakes. The team did not know what the exact pressure of work had been, but by checking their records on customer service demand and staff levels, they could make a pretty good estimate.

Turning to the issue of client acquisition, the team surmised that word had gotten around about their quality problems, and so their reputation had been tarnished. From the quality estimates and the contacts that people in their market might have had with each other, they estimated what might have happened to their firm's reputation. By putting this together with estimates of client losses, they obtained a picture of the dynamics of their client base (Exhibit 8.3).

The company's management was left with one puzzle. If client losses had risen so that workloads were falling, why had pressure on staff stayed so high? The decrease in workload should have brought things back into balance, and the problem should have fixed itself.

The company had maintained a strong hiring rate, but all the same, its staff numbers had gradually declined. Previously this had not been much of a problem because increasing experience kept productivity moving upward,

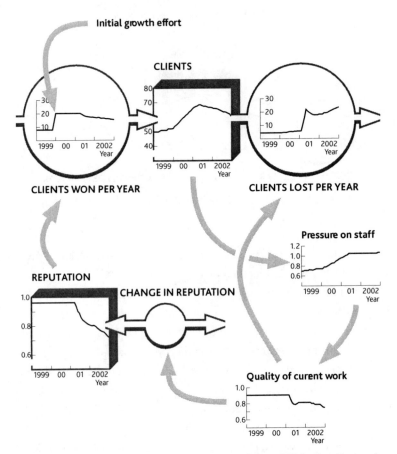

Exhibit 8.3. Pressure of Work Creates Problems With Quality and Reputation

but the benefit was not powerful enough to keep work pressure under control when all the new client business came in. Staff records showed that turnover had risen particularly sharply in the past year.

Strangely, the staff turnover problem appeared to be only a recent phenomenon. Conversations with some of the people leaving revealed that they were initially excited at the new opportunities coming in. It had taken time for the constant pressure of impossible demands to hit morale. The effect on motivation had been exacerbated by the now escalating need to refix the same client problems that should have been fixed before.

Doing It Right: Where Quality and Reputation Hit

Although we have to be careful not to force standard answers on a specific situation, the structure in Exhibit 8.3 is remarkably common. Current customers have direct experience of current quality, so they often respond quickly when problems arise. Potential customers, on the other hand, have no direct experience of your performance. They can only go on what they hear about you indirectly, from information that leaks out about you from existing customers. This process may be slow, depending on how often potential customers interact and the effectiveness of trade surveys, for example.

A further important point to note is that this firm felt its reputation was still declining even though quality was getting no worse. This is because continuing bad messages about quality persist in depleting reputation. So *current* quality often drives customer losses, while reputation (which reflects *past* quality) drives customer acquisition.

Sketching these phenomena on the board gave the team a clear picture of how the staff had been affected by recent events (Exhibit 8.4). They realized that their original hiring rate had never been high enough to build resilience in their group of professionals. Consequently, when pressure built up, the lid had blown off, which is why staff were now leaving at such a rapid rate.

Fixing the Problem

In this case, we can see two key groups (clients and staff) choosing to move from one state (with the firm) to another (*not* with it), each driven to make these choices by powerful intangible factors (quality, reputation, and morale). What could be done to fix this problem?

As long as reputation and morale remained weak, three important flows would continue to run against the firm: slow client acquisition and rapid staff and client losses. Since work pressure was driving these problems, this is where any solution would have to be applied. The obvious approach, hiring more staff, turned out to be the worst possible response. New people did not understand the clients' needs or how the organization's procedures

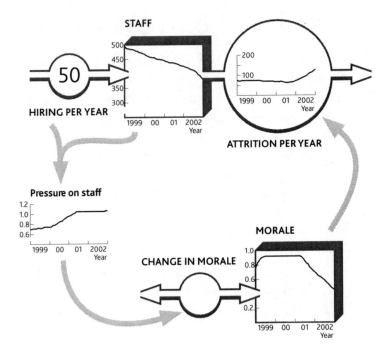

Exhibit 8.4. Work Pressure Hits Morale, So Staff Losses Escalate

worked. The already pressured staff had to work even harder to coach them. That left only one solution: cut the workload.

Less work meant fewer clients and perhaps less work from those that remained. The tough decision was made to terminate business from a selection of clients. Since the steady addition of new staff was also distracting the experienced staff, a further decision was made to stop hiring for the moment. However, certain types of work were subcontracted to another company.

The Significance of Counterintuitive Solutions

At first sight, this solution looks absurd: We are losing clients and having trouble winning new ones, so you want us to stop selling and actually *terminate* existing clients? Also, our staff is under too much pressure, so you want us to stop hiring?

In this case, "Yes" to both questions. The problems were being exacerbated by the very efforts designed to solve them. As ever, the critical question to ask was "What is driving the resource flows?" Only removing the source of the problems would reset the machine to a state where it could cope—although as you might imagine, this can be a tough case to sell.

Our service firm's perplexing response makes more sense when we look into the detail. First, the high ratio of work to capacity had one useful benefit: profits improved! This happy state was in danger of ending if the downturn continued, of course, but for now there was some financial headroom.

Second, the firm had some business that was more trouble than they were worth. Some clients constantly demanded more support than was in their original agreement. A selection of the worst offenders was called, told of the firm's difficulties, and asked to refrain from making all but the most urgent support requests while the problems were resolved. Others, including some of the firm's recent acquisitions, were advised to seek support elsewhere.

Third, client acquisition efforts did not cease altogether, but imminent potential business was just kept warm, rather than being actively sold a project. Indeed, the firm turned its response to its advantage, telling these clients that it was taking steps to fix the very problems about which they had heard rumors.

Beware! Just because dropping clients and freezing the hiring rate was right in *this* situation, it does not mean it will be right for you. A major implication of the strategy dynamics method is that simple solutions can rarely be transplanted from case to case (as is often implied for other management tools!). What is best for *you* depends on the specifics—including the numbers—in your own case.

The Growth and Decline of Intangible Resources

Just like the tangible resources discussed in earlier chapters, intangibles fill and drain away through time; that is what makes them resources. So once again we need to understand both how quickly this is happening and what is driving the flows. Reputation, for example, is raised by the frequency with which satisfied people tell others; staff motivation grows at a rate driven by events that make people feel good about working harder.

The more significant and frequent these events and experiences, the more the attitude is developed.

This buildup of positive commitment cannot go on for ever. A look at the service firm's early situation shows a reputation rating of nearly 1, and a limited buildup of morale among the developers. This is hardly surprising; there is only so much "feeling" you can push into people!

Influencing Intangible Resources

Managers can find ways to influence both the inflow and outflow of intangibles. Positive leadership behaviors, for example, encourage positive feelings among staff; confident statements about an organization's performance build commitment among investors or donors; and so on.

Skills training is a useful example, since it often comes with clear measurements (Tovey, 1994). Indeed, in many sectors, skills are routinely measured to ensure compliance with required standards. Exhibit 8.5 shows skills being built up by hours of training time but reaching limits in the trainees' ability to learn more. The framework distinguishes between the management action (amount of training given) and the impact it has on the resource that concerns us (increase in current skill level). We need this distinction in order to identify whether the effort is being effective. Indeed, we need to have *measures* for both items.

Although this may seem a rather mechanical view of how training works, something like this process goes on in real situations, and it does at least provide a way of making evidence-based judgments about management decisions. In practical cases, skills audits provide useful starting information and a firm's actual experience in training efforts yields good estimates of training impacts.

There are similarities, too, between the deterioration of tangible resources mentioned in chapter 3 and the decay of intangible resources. Skill levels drop if not maintained by practice or repeated training; employees can lose their enthusiasm for a job; donors may lose their commitment to supporting a charitable or political cause.

It is hardly surprising to see brands that are universally recognized and understood continuing to spend heavily on advertising. It is not just a matter of persuading newcomers to the market to become committed to

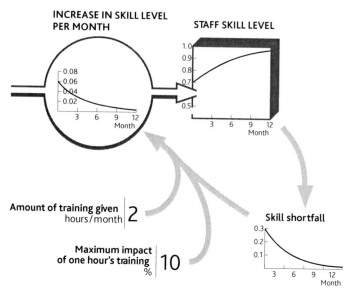

Exhibit 8.5. Building an Intangible Resource: Staff Skills

the brand, it is also vital to stop those who are already committed from losing their enthusiasm (Exhibit 8.6).

Expectations Build and Decay

Consider for a moment how reliable your current car has been since first you owned it (or consider a friend's car if you do not own one). How many times has it broken down in the past 30,000 miles? Twice maybe, or once, or perhaps not at all? Forty years ago, such reliability would have been rare, and your car would have been remarkable. Today, however, we have come to expect this level of reliability. This change has occurred because the more experience we have of exceptional reliability, the less exceptional it seems.

This phenomenon is important because it affects the way people respond to what you offer. Before these general improvements in vehicle reliability occurred, a company with a better than average performance could use that superiority to capture new customers. Now, that same company with that same reliability level has nothing to boast about.

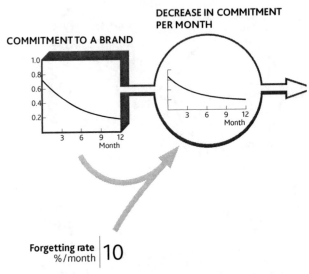

Exhibit 8.6. Decay in Commitment to a Brand

The Impact of Negative Perceptions

Unfortunately we often come up against problems caused by a different kind of feeling: a *negative* perception about something important. Customers and clients become irritated by repeated failures of products or services; staff get annoyed by repeated demands that they cannot fulfill. The consequences can be bizarre. For example, the public may become hostile to the police's efforts to enforce driving laws even though these laws exist to protect them from injury.

The same principles apply to negative as well as positive perceptions. In our service company example, you may recall that the staff's *positive* morale became more and more depleted. It is probable, though, that their *annoyance* increased to the point that they resigned. Indeed, both processes were probably going on at the same time. One part of their brain was reveling in the energy of constant intensive activity, while another part was getting angry about the pressure.

However, there is a limit or saturation point beyond which things can deteriorate no further. No one's brain cells, no matter how irate they are, can go on sending angry signals indefinitely. People become tired or bored and stop caring. We therefore need to think about and manage the balance between two countervailing mechanisms. On the one hand, we have customers, staff, or other stakeholders becoming more and more annoyed by a sequence of disappointing events. On the other hand, we have these same people losing the energy to keep being angry about them. If things carry on in this unsatisfactory manner as they are right now, these customers or staff reach an equilibrium level of dissatisfaction. They are not particularly satisfied, but neither are they so annoyed that they will do anything about it.

Intangibles Trigger Catastrophe

Earlier in this chapter I explained that intangibles drive two distinct behaviors among important groups that affect our performance. Intangibles result in us either *doing more or less* of something (serving customers better, recommending us more often to others, and so on) or else *switching* from one state to another (becoming a customer, employee, or investor, say). At a strategic level, we are often interested in the second possibility, since the overall behavior of large groups (such as clients, supporters, dealers, staff, or investors) reflects the sum of switching decisions made by each member of that group.

Our imaginary restaurant in earlier chapters relied on a large number of individual consumers deciding to become (or *stop* being) regular customers. Almost invariably, new consumers on a particular day had not spontaneously decided to become regular customers. It is much more likely that they become increasingly motivated to visit because of what they have heard about the restaurant, either from its marketing activity or from others.

The scale and frequency of received messages are likely to drive this buildup of state of mind until it triggers action. If our consumers had heard only sporadic and lukewarm recommendations, not enough motivation would have built up to spur them to action. Their brains needed a sufficiently strong push from new messages in order to overcome the depletion of their attention—their forgetting.

It is remarkably common for an increasing perception to build up to some trigger level that causes people to act. We work hard to persuade our people to try something new, but they just will not give it a go. We visit the same customer again and again, but we just cannot get them to sign that contract. We present paper after paper to the head office, but they just will not commit to the investment we want. Then all of a sudden, everything moves. Our people change the way they behave; the customer signs the contract; the head office approves our plan. It may even be some apparently trivial event that finally triggers the change.

The same phenomenon occurs with negative events too (Exhibit 8.7). Business may be running smoothly, with sales effort winning customers at a regular slow rate to replace the few who leave each month. Then problems crop up in customer service. They are small and infrequent at first, and because people can be tolerant they forgive and forget these little annoyances.

However, the service problems become more severe and frequent. Unknown to you, customers' annoyance is building up. Eventually so

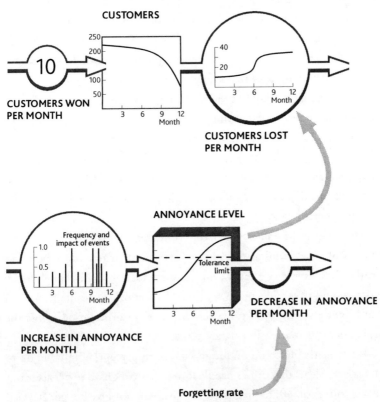

Exhibit 8.7. Customers React to a Trigger Level of Annoyance

much annoyance has accumulated that their tolerance threshold is breached, and losses increase. You have experienced what looks like a discontinuity, whereas in fact it is merely the crossover from *just* tolerable to unacceptable.

Similar mechanisms are widespread and cause a number of difficulties. The trouble that you eventually see (customer losses) is far removed from the original change that brought it about (service problems). As a result, you may have come to regard the situation as acceptable. After all, it has been going on for a long time with no harm, so why worry? The negative intangible stock (annoyance) is difficult—although not impossible—to detect and measure, and you may not even be conscious of the events that are filling it up. Even if you know about customers' poor experiences, it is hard to estimate how they interact with other things that affect their attitude, such as price or product performance.

There is nothing magical about deciding how to protect your organization from this kind of problem, although it can be difficult to judge whether the problem is important enough to justify the effort required. In particular, you need to

- be conscious of what range of issues are important to customers, especially those that become serious enough to prompt them to leave you;
- estimate how strongly people feel that things are not good enough. You need a sense of the range of events that could upset your customers, plus an idea of how badly different kinds of problems will upset them;
- understand how quickly they will forgive anything that goes wrong.

On the positive side, it is common for high annoyance levels to be rapidly reversed by remedial actions. In some cases, such a fix can even make customers feel better about you than if the problem had never arisen. Even so, I have not as yet found an organization that goes so far as to cause trouble for customers on purpose so it can give them the warm glow of having fixed it!

Finally, note that positive attitudes, too, can build to levels that trigger switching behavior that you *do* want. For example, good product reviews by lead customers build up a useful resource that other potential customers notice. If good reviews appear frequently enough, they can enable you to win new customers who would previously have been reluctant.

Capabilities: Activities You Are Good At

Capabilities are especially powerful drivers of performance for businesses and many other kinds of organization (Hamel & Heene,1994; Schoemaker, 1992; Stalk, Evans, & Schulman, 1992). They are the factors that determine how well groups achieve tasks that are critical. For our strategic architecture of resources, the most critical tasks include building and retaining resources. First, let us remind ourselves how capabilities differ from resources:

- Resources are useful *items* that you own or can access.
- Capabilities are *activities* that your organization is good at performing.

Capabilities are important because they determine how effectively your organization builds, develops, and retains resources. A more capable organization will be able to build resources *faster* and hold resource losses to a *slower* rate than a less capable organization. Capabilities, like intangible resources, are abstract and ambiguous items that are difficult to measure and manage. Nevertheless, they are important drivers of performance through time, so some attempt must be made to understand and manage them.

There are three useful reference points to bear in mind when you assess the strength of your capabilities for building resources:

1. **The maximum rate of resource building or retention**. For example, given good products and attractive prices, perfect sales capability would show up as a 100% hit rate in new customer acquisition.
2. **Best practice within the organization**. For example, if all our regional sales teams could build sales per customer as fast as region X does, how quickly would we grow sales?

3. **Benchmarks from firms in comparable sectors**. For example, if all our regional sales teams could build sales per customer as fast as competitor Y does, how quickly would we grow sales?

A team's capability is the ratio between the rate at which it is *actually* achieving tasks and the best rate that we can imagine, given one of the benchmarks above.

Skills Versus Capabilities

Do not confuse team capabilities with individual skills. If you wanted to evaluate the total skills of a group and assess its overall average skill at individual tasks, then you would use the idea of attributes from chapter 6. Clever organizations manage to take relatively unskilled people and generate outstanding performance. Consulting firms take newly trained professionals and enable them to deliver sophisticated business solutions; fast-food firms take unskilled staff and produce highly consistent products and service; call centers take people with little understanding of an organization's products and clients and produce excellent customer support; and so on.

Clearly such organizations achieve much of this performance by training people: in other words, by adding to their individual skills. But they do more: **They develop, test, and operate proven procedures**. Team capability, then, reflects the combination of individual skills and these effective procedures.

Such procedures add up to a library of instructions for completing specific activities quickly and reliably. This library is effectively a resource, something useful that you own, and like any resource it is built up over time. It is also kept up to date by the removal of obsolete or ineffective procedures and the addition of new ones. One of the clearest examples you are likely to find concerns the franchise manuals used by firms like McDonald's to both train their staff and control their franchisees. Such manuals cover everything from cleaning the fryers, to checking the inventory, to sorting the garbage.

Capabilities Accelerate Resource Development

As I have stressed before, if capabilities are to influence performance then it can *only* be by improving the organization's success at developing resources, whether it be winning them in the first place, promoting them from state to state, or retaining them. For example,

- a highly capable human resource (HR) team wins the people that the organization needs quickly, efficiently, and with the greatest likelihood that they will stay;
- a highly capable product development group turns out products quickly and cheaply that satisfy customers' needs;
- a highly capable customer support team ensures customers are content with the organization's products and services, thus preventing customer defection.

There is a limit to what capable teams can accomplish though if they do not have the resources to do their job. Even the best customer support group will struggle to keep customers if the products they are supporting are inadequate.

Learning, Capability Building, and Resource Development

The last mystery we need to resolve about capabilities is where they come from. Team capabilities are built up by being used, much as individual skills are. Procedures and methods for getting things done are available to be recorded whenever they take place. So techniques have been developed in many sectors for achieving a sale to a new customer, for example. Indeed, many of these techniques are common to multiple markets and embedded in sales force training systems. The procedures for managing products through a research and development (R&D) process similarly arise from companies' experience of actually carrying out that activity.

Clearly the more chances the team has to practice its winning, developing, and retention of resources, the more opportunities arise to test, improve, and record the procedures that work best. The bottom line is that the rate of resource *flows* determines the rate at which capabilities can be improved. If we add the earlier observation that capability *levels* drive resource flows, we have a simple and direct mutual reinforcement between each capability and the resource to which it relates. There are some cases where capability *does not* relate directly to a specific resource flow, but they tend to be less influential on long-term strategic performance than are these tightly coupled pairings of resource and capability.

Action Checklist: Managing the Impact of Intangibles on the Resource System

This chapter has explained the importance of intangible factors, given examples of simple measures for them, and shown you how they operate. Here are some techniques to ensure your intangibles are healthy and working well with the rest of your business system:

- **Identify the important intangibles.** Since your performance comes from concrete resources, start with these and ask whether an intangible factor is likely to influence your ability to win or lose them. However, do not go on an exhaustive search for as many soft factors as possible; each part of your strategic architecture will probably be most strongly influenced by one or two intangibles.
- **Be clear which of these soft factors genuinely accumulate through time and which are simply varying features of your organization.** "Quality" often reflects immediately the balance between what has to be done and what is available to do it, in which case it does not accumulate. Reputation, motivation, commitment, and perception, on the other hand, are built up and drain away over time in response to an entire history of events.
- **Specify intangibles carefully and identify the best measure.** What exactly is it that drives the choices of each group? That will be the measure that matters. Our IT service firm's *current* clients, for example, were strongly influenced by the error rate they experienced, while *potential* clients responded to the firm's reputation.

- **Identify the events causing each intangible to fill up and drain away.** This is the same bathtub principle we have used before, so remember that different items may be featured on either side of this question.
- **Look for places where you can strengthen intangibles.** If you were to lose some of your client relationship managers, for example, what could you do quickly to keep your reputation strong with the wider market and sustain the morale of your other staff?
- **Watch out for negative resources.** What can you do to slow down the unfortunate events that are filling up these negative feelings? Is there anything you can do to actively dissipate them?
- **Build intangible measures into your performance tracking system.** Reporting systems now commonly incorporate soft measures from various parts of the organization, recognizing that they are crucial to an effective system.
- **If you do not know, do not ignore the issue!** Soft factors *are* influencing your organization, continually and strongly. Remember that if you choose to ignore them, you are not actually leaving them out. Rather, you are assuming that they are OK and unchanging. This is unlikely to be the case, so make your best estimate and start tracking and understanding them.

Going Forward

This book has introduced the essential elements of the strategy dynamics approach to strategic management of businesses and other organizations. In an effort to make the ideas accessible to the widest possible range of people, I have kept the book short and the examples easy to follow. I have also simplified or left out many features and details of the approach while retaining the most powerful elements.

As with any methodical approach to management issues, it is much easier to make progress if everyone involved shares the same understanding, so it is helpful to develop a coalition of colleagues who have picked up the ideas and tried using them. Equally, it can be difficult to win support for new efforts when there is so much else going on around you. It is best to start small, perhaps using just one or two of the most useful frameworks from this book to work on specific challenges. As confidence grows, you can seek support for doing more.

There is much more to learn about how an organization's performance develops through time and how professional strategic management can drive big improvements to this trajectory.

- Another short book—my *Developing Employee Talent to Perform* (Business Expert Press, 2009)—provides guidance on how general managers and their teams can understand their organization's performance and drive it into the future. Those wishing to study the underlying method in more depth should see my book *Strategic Management Dynamics* (2008).
- The implications for marketing and brand strategy are well understood and have been put to good use in many businesses (see Lars Finskud, *Competing for Choice*, 2009).
- Learning materials, including a 10-class online course, simulation-based exercises, and worksheets, are available from Strategy Dynamics Ltd. at http://www.strategydynamics.com. These are designed for individual and team study, as well as for business school degree courses and executive training.

References

Bain & Company. (2007). *Management tools 2007: An executive's guide.* Retrieved November 15, 2008, from http://www.bain.com/management_tools/home .asp.

Barney, J. B. (2006). *Gaining and sustaining competitive advantage.* Reading, MA: Addison-Wesley.

Carmelli, A. (2004). Assessing core intangible resources. *European Management Journal, 22*(1), 110–122.

Christensen, C. M., & Raynor, M. (2003). Why hard-nosed executives should care about management theory. *Harvard Business Review, 81(9),* 66–75.

Collis, D. J., & Montgomery, C. A. (1994). Competing on resources: strategy in the 1990s. *Harvard Business Review, 74*(4), 118–128.

Copeland, T., Koller, T., & Murrin, J. (2000). *Valuation—measuring and managing the value of companies* (4th ed.). Chichester, UK: John Wiley & Sons.

Coyne, K., & Subramaniam, S. (2000). Bringing discipline to strategy. *McKinsey Quarterly, June Special Issue,* 61–70.

Desmet, D., Finskud, L., Glucksman, M., Marshall, N., Reyner, M., & Warren, K. (1998). The end of voodoo brand management? *McKinsey Quarterly, 2,* 106–117.

Dierickx, I., & Cool, K. (1989). Asset stock accumulation and sustainability of competitive advantage. *Management Science, 35,* 1504–1511.

Elling, M. E., Fogle, H. J., McKhann, C. S., & Simon, C. (2002). Making more of Pharma's sales force. *McKinsey Quarterly, 3,* 86–95.

Finskud, L. (2009). *Competing for choice.* Williston, VT: Business Expert Press.

Forrester, J. W. (1961). *Industrial dynamics.* Cambridge, MA: Productivity Press.

Grant, R. M. (2008). *Contemporary strategy analysis: Concepts, techniques, applications* (4th ed.). Oxford: Blackwell.

Hall, R. (1992). *The strategic analysis of intangible resources.* Chichester, UK: John Wiley & Sons.

Hamel, G., & Heene, A. (Eds.). (1994). *Competence-based competition.* Chichester, UK: John Wiley & Sons.

Kaplan, R. S., & Norton, D. P. (1996). *The balanced scorecard: Translating strategy into action.* Cambridge, MA: Harvard Business School Press.

Keough, M., & Doman, A. (1992). The CEO as organizational designer: An interview with Prof. Jay W. Forrester. *McKinsey Quarterly, 2,* 3–30.

McDonald's Corporation. (2003). 2002 Summary Annual Report. McDonald's Corporation: Oak Brook, IL. Page 1. Retrieved March 13, 2009, from http://www.mcdonalds.com/corp/invest/pub/annual_rpt_archives/2002_annual.html

Mainardi, C., Leinwand, P., & Lauster, S. (2008). How to win by changing the game. *Strategy + Business, 53*, 22–28.

McGahan, A., & Porter, M. E. (1997). How much does industry matter, really? *Strategic Management Journal, 18*(Summer Special Issue), 15–30.

Mintzberg, H., Lampel, J. B., Quinn, J. B., & Ghoshal, S. (1997). *The strategy process* (4th ed.). London: Prentice-Hall.

Porter, M. E. (1980). *Competitive strategy*. New York: Free Press.

Prahalad, C. K. (2006). *The fortune at the bottom of the pyramid*. Upper Saddle River, NJ: Pearson.

Schoemaker, P. J. H. (1992). How to link strategic vision to core capabilities. *Sloan Management Review, 34*(1), 67–81.

Stalk, G., Evans, P., & Shulman, L. (1992). Competing on capabilities. *Harvard Business Review, 70*(2), 57–69.

Sterman, J. D. (2000). *Business dynamics*. New York: Irwin McGraw-Hill.

Tovey, L. (1994). Competency assessment: A strategic approach—Part II. *Executive Development, 7*(1), 16–19.

Warren, K. D. (2008). *Strategic management dynamics*. Chichester, UK: John Wiley & Sons.

Warren, K. D. (2009). *Developing employee talent to perform*. New York: Business Expert Press.

Index

Note: The italicized *e* or *t* following page numbers refers to exhibits or tables, respectively.

A
airlines, 14, 21, 23–27, 25*e*, 26*e*, 70–72, 71*e*, 79, 87
Alibaba.com, 5–6, 5*e*, 10*t*
arrows in diagrams, 55
assessing resource quality, 83–89, 84*e*
attributes. *See* resource attributes

B
Blockbuster Inc., 6–8, 7*e*, 10*t*
building strategic architecture, 66–77, 66*e*–69*e*
business
 language, 49
 resources within, 39–40, 40*e*
business leader challenge, 3–4

C
calculating average attributes, 92
capabilities, intangible resources, 128–31
checking for reinforcing feedback, 58–59
choice chain, 41–43, 42*e*
coflow structure, resource attributes, 89–93, 91*e*
collapse, and interdependence between resources, 57–58
competing
 for potential customers, 99, 100*e*–101*e*
 for rivals' customers, 101–4, 102*e*
 for sales to shared customers, 104–6, 105*e*
competitive dynamics, 106–9, 107*e*
complementary resources, 20–21, 56, 78
conserving resources, 40, 40*e*

constrained growth and interdependence, 59–62, 59*e*–61*e*
control management, strategic architecture, 78–82
copying ease, resources, 20
counterintuitive solutions, intangible resources, 120–21

D
decisions, resource flows and, 46–48, 47*e*–48*e*
decline, intangibles, 121–28
defining resources, 23–30
demand-side resources, 27–28
developing resources, 38–44, 38*e*
diagnosing performance, 15, 15*e*
diagrams, 22*e*, 23, 24*e*
 arrows in, 55
Disney Princess dolls, 98–107
drivers, resource flow rates, 56
driving growth in others, resources, 51–56, 53*e*–55*e*
durable resources, 20
dynamic market intelligence rivalry, 104

E
existing resources, 51–56, 53*e*–55*e*
external resources, 38–39

F
feedback, reinforcing, 51–59, 52*e*
fill and drain resources, 31–33, 32*e*–34*e*
financial resources, 29–30
fixing problems
 intangibles, 119–20
 strategic architecture, 75–78

G

gaining resources, 45–51
growth, intangible resources, 121–28
growth stimulation resources, 51–52,
    52e

I

identifying resources, 21–23, 22e
industry analysis and strategy, 9–11
inflows, outflows and, 37
influencing intangibles, 122–23, 123e
intangible resources, 111–32. *See also*
    resources
  capabilities, 128–31
  counterintuitive solutions, 120–21
  expectations, 123–24, 124e
  fixing problems, 119–20
  growth and decline, 121–28
  importance of, 111–12
  influencing, 122–23, 123e
  IT service firm, 116–19, 117e, 118e
  measuring, 112–16, 113e
  negative perceptions, 124–28, 126e
  problems caused by soft factors,
      116–21, 117e, 118e, 120e
  quality and reputation problems,
      118e, 119, 120e
  quality as, 115
  skills, 129
interdependence
  collapse, 57–58
  constrained growth, 59–62,
      59e–61e
  leveraging, 62–63
  between resources, 45–63
IT service firm, 116–19, 117e, 118e

L

language, business, 49
leveraging interdependence, 62–63

M

Ma, Jack, 5
maintaining resources, 45–51
management control of resources,
    34–37, 35e–37e
management tools, problems with,
    8–9

managing
  resource attributes, 89–93, 91e
  rivalry for customers and other
      resources, 97–109
  strategic architecture, 65–82
Massachusetts Institute of Technology, 1
Mattel Barbie doll, 98–107
measuring resources, 23–30
MECE, 40, 40e
mobile resources, 20

N

negative perceptions about intangible
    resources, 124–28, 126e
Netflix, 10
nonbusiness settings, 13–14, 13e

O

other resource growth, 50–51
outflows, inflows and, 37

P

performance through time, 3–17
performance time path, 16–17
political, economic, social, and
    technological (PEST) analysis, 9,
    48–50
problems
  caused by soft factors for intangi-
      bles, 116–21, 117e, 118e, 120e
  quality and reputation, 118e, 119,
      120e
  with resource attributes, 93–94

Q

quality
  assessing, 83–89, 84e
  problems, 118e, 119, 120e
  as resource for intangibles, 115
quantity as resource for intangibles,
    83–95

R

reinforcing feedback, 51–59, 52e
  checking for, 58–59
  limits and pitfalls, 57
reputation problems, intangibles,
    118e, 119, 120e

resource attributes
  calculating average attributes, 92
  coflow structure, 89–93, 91*e*
  managing, 89–93, 91*e*
  problems with, 93–94
  thinking about, 90
resource-based view (RBV), 9
resource flows
  and decisions, 46–48, 47*e*–48*e*
  outside forces effect, 48–50
  rates, 56
resources, 21. *See also* intangible
    resources
  airlines, 23–27, 25*e*, 26*e*
  assessing quality, 83–89, 84*e*
  within business, 39–40, 40*e*
  conserving, 40, 40*e*
  copying ease, 20
  defining, 23–30
  demand-side, 27–28
  developing, 38–44, 38*e*
  drive growth in others, 51–56,
    53*e*–55*e*
  as drivers of performance, 19–30
  durable, 20
  existing, 51–56, 53*e*–55*e*
  external, 38–39
  fill and drain, 31, 32*e*–34*e*
  financial, 29–30
  gaining, 45–51
  identifying, 21–23, 22*e*
  maintaining, 45–51
  management control, 34–37,
    35*e*–37*e*
  measuring, 23–30
  mobile, 20
  and other resource growth, 50–51
  standard types, 27
  stimulate growth, 51–52, 52*e*
  substitutability, 20
  supply-side, 28–29
  tradable, 20
  value, 19–21

rivalry
  about, 97–98
  competing for potential customers,
    99, 100*e*–101*e*
  competing for rivals' customers,
    101–4, 102*e*
  competing for sales to shared cus-
    tomers, 104–6, 105*e*
  competitive dynamics, 106–9, 107*e*
  Disney Princess dolls, 98–107
  dynamic market intelligence, 104
  managing, 97–109
  Mattel Barbie doll, 98–107
  types, 97–106
Ryanair, 14, 21, 26, 26*e*, 87

S
skills, as intangibles, 129
Southwest Airlines, 14, 21, 87
strategic architecture
  building, 66–77, 66*e*–69*e*
  control management, 78–82
  fixes, 75–78
  using, 70–75, 71*e*, 75*e*
strategy dynamics, 1–2
substitutability of resources, 20
supply-side resources, 28–29
SWOT analysis, 9, 10*t*

T
time, importance, 4–8
time path, 11–13
tradable resources, 20

U
using strategic architecture, 70–75,
    71*e*, 75*e*

V
value
  of performance, 15–16
  of resources, 19–21